# Computer Networking

*An All-in-One Beginner's Guide to Understanding Communications Systems, Network Security, Internet Connections, Cybersecurity and Hacking*

# Contents

# Introduction

This book is a concoction of several computer topics that are relevant and popular in the modern age. Throughout this book, the reader will explore each topic with easy-to-understand terminology and analogies. The book starts with a descriptive and comprehensive insight into computer networking and then branches off to cover network security, network designing, and hacking. The delivery of topics is specifically designed to:

- Entertain the needs of the readers.
- Provide valuable insights into the world of computer networking in the modern era.
- Deliver elaborative yet to-the-point knowledge.

Once the computer networking portion of this book is finished, the reader will be greeted with the other topics in this all-in-one guide. In the ending section, there is an informative description of the kill-chain process in hacking. This topic is not only interesting but also informative and refers to the methods hackers employ when penetrating target systems and networks. So, buckle your seatbelts and enjoy the ride.

# Chapter 1: Computer Networking Basics

In this chapter, we will explore the fundamentals and the very basic concepts of computer networking. By doing so, we will essentially lay a conceptual foundation for the reader. This will help increase the digestibility of the later discussed concepts and some technical details of computer networking.

Hence, this chapter will be primarily focused on emphasizing the basic details of computer networking and then steadily building upon the knowledge as you learn.

To start things off, we will go through a brief introduction of what computer networking actually is. Then we will delve deeper into the details solidifying the understanding of each concept that the reader will have successfully learned.

## What is Modern Computer Networking?

The word "networking" describes a connection or set of connections between multiple objects. Similarly, "computer networking" refers to the interconnection of two or more computers together to allow for sharing resources. A network of computers can be established in a variety of environments, such as homes, offices, or even in large business organizations. Computer networking stretches even to the international scope where computers are connected through the Internet. A more subtle and easily observed example of computer networking is a printer or a scanner connected (wired or wireless) to the user's personal computer.

Since the fundamental purpose of computer networking is to interconnect different PCs, an interesting question arises; why do we need computer networking in the first place?

The answer to this is very simple. If a person wants to watch a movie, a video, or even a talk show, he can do so in two ways.

- By having a physical storage device that contains the content, viewable on his computer, or simply by hopping onto the Internet and accessing the website where he can find the content and view it directly from there.

- The latter approach involves computer networking. It enables the viewer to connect to a remote computer server that is the host of the website allowing the visitor to use its resources to view his favorite content. This is just a simple example of how computer networking benefits an average user.

The phenomenon of the Internet is a by-product of computer networking, and we all know what it's like to spend a few days without the Internet. While we have discussed how big a deal computer networking is to a common person, it becomes even more important and crucial for big organizations and institutes such as hospitals, business companies, law enforcement departments, etc. These organizations rely on computer networking to:

- Efficiently establish an information channel through which the entire organization communicates the data being gathered and modified. Computer networking has a huge influence on not only the professional sector but also the business sector as well because, without a proper networking infrastructure, the respective industry would essentially just collapse.

Hence, to understand the importance and the very basic function of computer networking, note that computer networking is the very foundation of the Internet itself.

Transferring data from one place to another is the purpose of networking. Another important thing we have to know about any connection is how much data it can carry from one place to another. This capacity to carry data is called *bandwidth*. If a connection has a higher capacity bandwidth, it can carry more data within a specific time slot.

The rate at which a network can transfer data is measured in bits per second, which are abbreviated as 'Bps.' Bps means how many bits a bandwidth can carry per second. In the modern age, computer technology and networking have come a long way; this bandwidth capacity is now measured in multiples of thousands. The different measures of data transfer speed are:

- Kilobytes - thousands of bits per second (Kbps)
- Megabytes - millions of bits per second, or thousands of Kilobytes per second (Mbps)
- Gigabytes - billions of bits per second, or thousands of Megabits per second (Gbps)

A closely related measurement you will also see in computer networking is 'hertz'; it is the number of cycles being carried per second, in the same way 'hertz' expresses the number of cycles per second in an alternating-current signal. Hertz is abbreviated as 'Hz' and is used to measure the computational speed of a processor. This measurement is taken in multiples of thousands, and:

- A thousand Hertz is known as a kilohertz (kHz)
- A million Hertz is known as a Megahertz (MHz)
- A billion Hertz is known as a Gigahertz (GHz)

For example, a processor running at 100 MHz means 100 million cycles per second. Hz and bps are essentially the same measurement but used for different elements. However, sometimes they can be mixed up. For instance, saying that an Ethernet cable supports a 10 MHz bandwidth instead of 10 Mbps is acceptable in common usage.

# Chapter 2: Networking Services Explained

In this section, we will discuss several network protocols that either rely on or make use of the TCP/IP protocol.

The protocols we will be discussing are listed below

   1.DNS
   2.DHCP
   3.HTTP
   4.FTP
   5.NNTP
   6.SMTP

There will be references to the levels at which these protocols operate in terms of the Open Systems Interconnection, or "OSI", networking model. The OSI model defines most methods and protocols through which computers connect and communicate with each other on a network. It is an abstract visualization, but a useful one; understanding the OSI networking model will create a strong foundation for network designing and network solution engineering.

Chapter Six goes into a detailed treatment of the topic, but, purely for the sake of reference between here and there, we will merely present here a basic outline of the OSI model.

The model is divided into seven distinct and separate layers. Each layer possesses a trait known as 'successive dependence.' This means that the successively higher layers in the model depend largely on the services and characteristics of the preceding lower layers.

Consider a standard desktop computer system. It is composed of several components that must work together to make the system functional. If we divide this system into the layers of the OSI networking model, the hardware components of this computer will be termed as the 'lowest layer.' The next layer above the hardware layer of this computer would be the Operating System and its system drivers.

Obviously, the operating system and drivers would be useless without the corresponding hardware. Hence, this higher layer is depending on the preceding lower layer to perform its function properly. This successive-hierarchy visualization continues upwards to the final layer, where an application is displaying useful and digestible data to the user.

The seven layers of the OSI Networking Model are:

1. **Physical Layer** - The physical layer specifies the network cable, the router, the

> DSU/CSU box, and the other physical mediums involved.

2. **Data Link Layer** - The data link layer of the OSI model bridges the connection

> between the third layer (network layer) and the first layer
> (physical layer) by defining and implementing a protocol

through which the network layer transmits its data to the
physical layer.

3. **Network Layer** – The main job of the network layer is to define the route through

which the data packets will travel from node to node. For this

purpose, the transport layer masks the characteristics of lower

layers from the upper layers in the OSI model.

4. **Transport Layer** – The transport layer mediates the movement of data between all

the other layers.

5. **Session Layer** – By this layer, the OSI model defines the connection between two

computers as either a client-server connection or a peer-t0-peer

connection. The term 'session' is used to describe this virtual

network connection between computers.

6. **Presentation Layer** – The presentation layer performs data compression/

decompression and
encryption/decryption.

7. **Application Layer** – The main concern of the application layer is to control and

mediate the interaction of the network with the Operating

System and the applications installed on this OS. It basically

defines how the applications handle the communications in

which the system becomes involved when connected to a

network.

If we analyze the nature of the OSI-model layers in a network, we see that they begin their interaction with the physical elements within a network, i.e., the routers, network cables, etc. From there, the layers move toward interacting with virtual features and elements, i.e., moving toward intelligent aspects of the network. After this, the OSI model's focus on the virtual aspects of the network shift towards the involvement of the computer machine itself within the network, which is evident from the last two layers (Presentation and Application layers).

A good grasp of this technique allows network engineers to analyze networks in a more detailed and comprehensive manner.

# Domain Name System (DNS)

The Doman Name System was developed to solve the inherent problem of keeping track of websites' IP addresses on the Internet. For instance, let's say that you want to visit Google. If the server housing Google's resources had only an IP address, then you would have to type in **http://209.85.171.100** to access it. If the computer addresses on the Internet had the same addressing scheme, keeping track of them would be very difficult.

This is where DNS comes in. By using this system, people can register a name for their domain with ICANN. This registered name will access that IP address on the Internet. Here are some of the common domain extensions:

- **.edu** (used by educational institutions)
- **.gov** (used by governmental institutions)
- **.mil** (used by military institutions)
- **.net** (used by entities related to the Internet)
- **.org** (used by non-profit organizations)
- **.xx** (used by countries. The "xx" is a space-holder and is replaced by the respective country's initials. For instance, for America: ".us").

Once an entity has acquired a domain name, it may add descriptors into the domain name. For instance, for the domain **dirbs.gov**, the government entity can add **pta.dirbs.gov,** and it would be acceptable.

The names of the domains are resolved to their respective IP addresses by using DNS servers, which means 'domain-name servers'. These servers perform a database query against a domain name entered by the user. The server then returns the actual address of the domain to the user's web browser.

# Dynamic Host Configuration Protocol (DHCP)

The DHCP protocol was developed to facilitate the administrators of a network to assign TCP/IP addresses to nodes easily. This protocol was used in a time when administrators would resolve the address of a node to a TCP/IP address and put it into a text file or even a dialog box.

The services given by the DHCP protocol is essentially run by dedicated servers known as DHCP servers. These servers control a 'scope,' which is an array of IP addresses. So, when a node goes online on a network, it requests the DHCP server to assign it an address. These addresses are valid for a limited period and expire after the time limit assigned; they then become available for another node to use. This period is known as the 'lease period,' and it can be set by the administrators of the network.

The main use of the DHCP protocol is to support the connectivity needs of client workstations. Using DHCP for the nodes responsible for network services is not recommended, as any change to the TCP/IP address will negate the connection to the network service.

# Hypertext Transfer Protocol (HTTP)

The entire Internet (called the World Wide Web) is a collection of documents created using a formatting language known as 'HTML' or 'Hypertext Markup Language.' Hypertexts on the Internet usually consist of:

- Displayed text
- Graphical images
- Formatting commands
- Hyperlinks (clicking them redirects the user to some other document on the Internet)

HTML documents are commonly accessed by using web browsers such as Google, Chrome, and Safari.

The Hypertext Transfer Protocol is what controls the transfer of data between the client and the webserver. This protocol operates at the application layer of the OSI model. The HTTP protocol makes use of other Internet protocols and DNS to establish a connection between the web client and the webserver. The HTTP protocol itself is insecure because transferring data happens with no encryption and can be intercepted. To resolve this security issue, we now use 'HTTP secure', commonly known as HTTPS, and SSL (Secure Socket Layers).

# File Transfer Protocol (FTP)

The word FTP refers to both 'File Transfer Protocol' and 'File Transfer Program,' both of which are related to each other in that the latter is an application that makes use of the FTP protocol. However, in this section, we will only discuss the FTP protocol.

FTP performs at the application layer in the OSI model, and it defines the method by which file data is sent and received between the FTP client and the FTP server. The data transferred can be text-based or binary-based, and there is no limit on the file size FTP can handle.

To perform a file transfer, the user must first connect to the FTP server and log in with a valid username and password. Some sites allow users to enter the username 'anonymous' with their e-mail address being the password. This is known as 'Anonymous FTP.'

# Network News Transfer Protocol (NNTP)

This protocol is specifically used for Usenet. Usenet is a term referring to discussion groups on the Internet. These groups cover a huge variety of topics, and at the moment, there over ten thousand Usenet groups on the Internet. The conversations of a Usenet group are sent to the Usenet servers, which are then sent to the other international Usenet servers by echoing.

Several classifications of Usenet groups are:

- **Alt:** Usenet group that focuses on topics on alternate lifestyles and miscellaneous issues.
- **Comp:** Usenet group that focuses on computer topics.
- **Gov:** Usenet group that focuses on discussions about governments.
- **Rec:** focus on recreational topics.
- **Sci:** focus on discussions about science.

Usenet groups are not all public. Those groups that are public get the news echoed by other Usenet servers, but the private ones are generally hosted by some organization or institution. Private Usenet groups require users to authenticate themselves with proper usernames and passwords.

The phenomenon of Usenet is made possible only by the NNTP protocol. This protocol establishes a connection between the Usenet server and the Usenet reader. The protocol also handles message formatting. This makes it possible for the messages to be text-based or carry binary attachments. Messages with binary attachments are encoded through MIME, or Multipurpose Internet Message Encoding (the same encoder used for e-mail attachments).

# Simple Mail Transfer Protocol (SMTP)

The Simple Mail Transfer Protocol handles the sending and receiving of e-mails from one e-mail server to another. The SMTP protocol is simply a way to communicate with the sending and receiving systems of e-mail servers.

The SMTP protocol comes into play when the system sending the e-mail message connects to the receiving system through port 25. Once the connection between the two systems has been established, the sender then transmits a '**HELO**' command along with its respective address towards the receiving system. Once this command has been acknowledged, and the receiver responds with its own address, then communication is initiated. The sender can then issue a command indicating it wants to send a message, by specifying the intended recipient of the message. Once the receiving system gets this request, it looks for the recipient. If the recipient is known to the system, then the request is acknowledged, and the sending system then forwards the message, along with any attachments, to the recipient. Once the receiving system has acknowledged that the entire message has been received, it terminates the connection.

# Keeping the Networks Safe with Firewalls

Most people reading this book would have come across the Windows firewall prompt at least once. This firewall application running on your machine is what keeps the network security policies upheld. Firewalls are hardware devices that protect a network by enforcing the network's security policies. In most networks, a firewall is installed into the router itself, leveraging its micro-processing chip and built-in memory. This is true with networks designed and installed in small offices or similar scenarios. However, for large networks, the networking equipment includes dedicated hardware running the firewall. This hardware can be a single unit or multiple pieces.

Normally, a separate computer running the firewall software is designated for the network. Otherwise, there can be a firewall device with a computer chip within it. Generally, a firewall acts as an outpost stationed between a LAN and the Internet. Regarding the firewalls available for use, there are mainly two types:

1. **Network-Based Firewall:** This firewall operates at the third layer, also known as the data-link layer, of the OSI networking model. The security technique used by a network-based firewall is primarily 'packet filtering.' Using this technique, the firewall is programmed with a defined set of rules. Whenever data packets travel between the two networks, the firewall analyzes and compares this packet against the rules and then decides whether the packet should be allowed to arrive or depart from the network or not. The permission or denial of passage according to the packet-filtering rules for the data packets is usually based on their destination address, source address, or the TCP/IP port.

2. **Application Based Firewall:** This firewall serves the role of a proxy. The word 'proxy' in this context means that the firewall represents the user's interactive session with the server of which services are requested. An application-based firewall allows no data traffic to pass through the two networks directly. Instead, the

communication between the two networks will be handled on one side by the firewall, as a proxy. This is why an application-based firewall is also known as a 'proxy firewall.' The technique used by a proxy firewall is 'NAT,' also known as 'Network Address Translation.' In this technique, the main idea is to conceal the network addresses of the internal network so it is not directly visible to the external network. In an application-based model, the firewall is responsible for the transmission of data to the network addresses for which the connections are established.

# Chapter 3: Getting into the Networking Hardware Fundamentals of Computer Relationships

The term 'computer relationship' refers to how a computer interacts with another computer connected on a network. There are generally two types of computer relationship.

1. Peer to Peer
2. Client/server

These two types of relationships essentially define the logical structure of a network. To understand them better, make an analogy to different management philosophies.

A peer-to-peer, or 'P2P', network is much like a decentralized management philosophy where decisions are made locally, and resources are managed according to what users need to do first.

A Client/server network is almost like a company that uses centralized management where decisions are made in a central location within a group of a few people. There exist circumstances where P2P and client/server relationships are both appropriate, and many networks incorporate both in their setup.

Both P2P and client/server networks need certain layers in the OSI model to be common, along with a physical network connection between the communicating computers using the same network protocols. In this respect, the two types of computer relationships are virtually the same in a network. However, the major difference arises from whether you spread the shared network resources around all the computers on the network or use the centralized network servers.

## Core Hardware Elements of a Network

To reinforce and solidify the foundation of the concepts we are exploring in this discussion, you must learn more about the physical hardware components that make up a computer network. Until now, we have focused more on how a network works and interacts on the virtual level rather than the physical level. However, by understanding the behavior of the network in its virtual realm, we are now set up to understand the hardware.

Understanding the physical aspect of computer networks provides us with adequate knowledge by which we can not only set up a computer network properly but also troubleshoot and maintain it.

In this section we will be discussing the following hardware, each a core component of the network:

1. Servers
2. Hubs
3. Routers
4. Switches
5. Cabling and cable plants
6. Workstation hardware

In the ending sections of this chapter, we will discuss these hardware components within the context of directing network traffic.

However, we will only focus on understanding these components and their purposes.

# Servers

A server is a computer assigned a very important and demanding job in computer networking. A server computer is essentially the component that handles all the networking requests and other functions of the computers on the network. Based on the network functions, a server can be classified into these different categories.

- **File and Print Servers:** This category includes those servers that primarily provide file-sharing services to other computers, and handle requests for network-based printers.

- **Application Servers:** The servers that essentially provide specific network application services to programs and software fall under this category. For example, a server running a database can provide (on request) access to the database to a distributed application connected to this server.

- **E-mail Servers:** The servers primarily designed to store e-mails and provide interconnection services to the corresponding clients are categorized as 'E-mail Servers.'

- **Networking Servers:** This category of servers mainly offers a variety of services related to networking. For example, a DHCP server programmed to assign TCP/IP addresses is categorized as a networking server. Similarly, a server handling the routing of data packets through different networks (routing server), is providing a network service and is hence categorized as a network server. Other such services performed by network servers include encryption, decryption, security access, and VPN access services.

- **Internet Servers:** The servers that provide access to common Internet services such as the World Wide Web,

Usenet News (NNTP), or even e-mail services based on the Internet, are known as Internet servers.

- **Remote Access Servers:** Such types of servers generally serve as a gateway or access point for users that want to access a network remotely.

An operating system installed on a server is very specific and tailored to enable the performance of the tasks we have just mentioned. For instance, if a server is using an operating system distributed by Microsoft, then it will most likely be using the Windows Server edition. Such operating systems come pre-loaded with networking software. Similarly, a server can also run Linux or UNIX distributions designed for networking. Depending on the operating system installed, a server can either perform the networking functions or be specific to only a few. But it's not always necessary for a server to comply with every network function; depending on its purpose, a server can only be tasked with a few networking operations, and that will be adequate. In this way, users can deploy multiple servers, each optimized for certain network operations.

Here are a few features that qualify a server for a different class of computers as compared to domestic client computers.

- Server computers natively incorporate the element of redundancy inside their hardware architecture. This means that even if something within the hardware breaks or fails, the server will still keep running normally. To achieve this redundancy, the internals of a server computer are lined with multiple power supplies and cooling fans, shielding the computer from malfunctioning due to the failure of any corresponding hardware component.

- The subsystems of a server computer are also specifically designed to optimize data flow. If we analyze a typical server, we will see that the design scheme for the disk, memory, and network subsystems are different than those used for a desktop computer. This design supports a high-performance boost to not only the subsystems mentioned above but also to optimize the flow of data. So, data moving to and from different points such as the server, the client, and the network is comparatively more optimized and faster.

• Since servers hold a crucial position within a computer network, special care is taken for the "health" of the computer. Server computers feature specially designed surveillance parameters on both software and hardware levels; the machine itself can keep an eye out for any alarming deterioration in its health and essentially warn the users of imminent failure before it happens. For instance, one of the common monitoring items installed in servers is temperature monitors; if the temperature of the server's surroundings rises too much, it gives off a warning detailing the problem. In this way, the people maintaining the server learn of a problem before it causes hardware failure and can prioritize resolving this issue.

## Hubs, Switches, and Routers

The purpose of hardware components such as hubs, switches, and routers is purely to facilitate the establishment and proper functioning of a network. Hence, these three components are 'pure' networking hardware and categorized under the class of 'internetworking devices.' These components are essentially the foundation of any basic or complex network, as the entire cabling system in a network is connected to these devices. In terms of the OSI networking model, the data flow from these devices can be defined at the physical, data link, or even the network layer.

Let's talk about **hubs** first. Hubs are also commonly called 'concentrators.' The core purpose of a hub provides a point of central connection for the network cables. Hubs can support multiple network cables; the number of cables is a matter of the hub's size. A typical small hub can connect network cables coming from two computers while a large hub can support over sixty computers (depending on the specification). The most popular hub is neither 'small' nor 'large', but a 'medium-sized' hub that generally supports up to 24 client computers.

In a hub, there is a logical wire through which the connected client computers communicate with the network. The capability of this logical wire is known as the 'collision domain.' Sometimes, interference results when too many client computers are connected to a single hub and attempt to communicate with the network.

We will now discuss **switches**. The circuital infrastructure (how the wires have been arranged) of a switch is strikingly similar to that of a hub. A switch also looks similar to a hub. Although the conceptual foundation of the working of hubs and switches are also very similar, the similarity ends there. Unlike the hub, each connection port on a switch has its own collision domain. In this way, each network connection on a switch can freely communicate with the network through a separate collision domain rather than a single one.

Each network connection on a switch is made to be a private connection. Nowadays, most computer networks implement switches instead of hubs, mainly because they are a cheaper solution. However, switches also have numerous benefits over hubs (we'll leave this discussion for some other time since the main focus is to learn how they work). Good network solutions will use one or more backbone switches, which connect to the main switch(es). These backbone switches generally operate at a speed much higher than the main switch(es). However, even if hubs are used in a network solution, there will still be the use of a backbone switch (which is simply an individual switch connected to the hub). The figure below shows a typical arrangement of switches and hubs in a network.

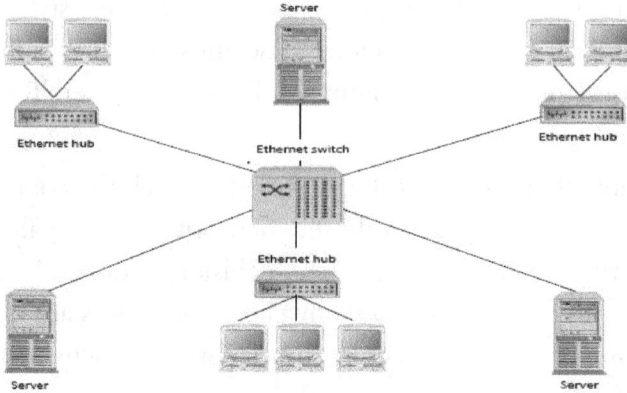

Last but not least, the **router**. By now, we have given adequate attention to the details of how a router works and functions. We now know that the primary job of a router in a computer network is to route the data packets effectively through one network on to the next. A router can also be a bridge that offers a path of flow for the data packets between two connected networks. These two networks establish a connection to the router by using their respective types of wiring and connection.

Let's understand this better through an example. Consider a router in a network that establishes a connection between a 10Base-T network and an ISDN telephone line. In this scenario, the router is dealing with two network connections, one from/to the 10Base-T network and the other from/to the ISDN telephone line. The job of the router will be to create a proper route for the data packets to travel between these two network connections.

Besides these defined network connections, the router can also have another terminal connection. The purpose of this secondary connection would be to program and maintain the router itself.

# Cabling and Cable Plants

When setting up a computer network, you'll find there is a huge variety of network cables available to use. But on this level, we should only concern ourselves with the main network cables commonly used.

The most common network cable used while setting up a Local Area Network connection is the Category 5 twisted-pair cables. These cables are also called 'Cat-5' cables. The cable has four twisted pairs; this means it has eight wire contact points. Due to this design, the cable can carry the network signal to each of these eight wire points. The Category 5 twisted-pair network cable is primarily used with Base-T networks such as the 100Base-T network and the 1000Base-T Ethernet network.

A lower-grade version of this same network cable is also available, and it is termed 'the Category 3 twisted-pair cable'. The overall design and structure of the network cable are similar to that of the higher-end Cat-5 cable; the main difference is the number of pairs it supports. While the Cat-5 cable has four twisted pairs of wires, the Cat-3 cable has two twisted pairs of wires, i.e., half of the Cat-5. Hence, the Cat-3 twisted-pair network cable is generally used to support older network connections such as the 10Base-T network and uses connectors comparatively smaller than the Cat-5 connectors.

Similarly, there are newer and improved versions of the Category 5 twisted-pair cables available now. There is the improved Cat-5E cable and the new Cat-6 standard network cable. There isn't much difference between the Cat-5 and the newer versions; the Cat-5E and Cat-6 are essentially the same as Cat-5 cables. The only difference is these newer twisted-pair network cables support higher network specifications, making them ideal for installation in networks running at higher speeds. Since there's little physical difference, the newer versions are backward compatible with the older network types. If you used Cat-5 cable for a 100Base-T network, then you can also the Cat-5E and Cat-6 network cables for the same network connections.

Another type of network cable popular in the past but is not so common for newer network installations nowadays is the **coaxial cable**. This cable can be found installed in old network installations in old buildings.

Let's talk about the structure of the coaxial cable. In this network cable, there is a central core, usually no more than a thick wire, made up of copper and known as the 'conductor.' This core is surrounded by a plastic material. This plastic cover over the conductor is wrapped with a 'shield' which is basically braided metal. Over this shield, there is an outer covering made out of plastic. Back in the day, you might have seen a thick cable that would connect your television set to the TV cable station's network. This cable was also a type of coaxial cable, and this same cable was also used for cable modems as well in the olden days. The particular coaxial cable used in networks such as 'Thin Ethernet' or 10Base-2 was the RG-58 coaxial cable.

Similarly, for networks such as ARCnet, another (but similar) coaxial cable would be used, which was the RG-56 coaxial cable. The coaxial cable to be used would depend on the specification of the network in which it was being installed. A network's specifications would define the support for a certain type of coaxial cable. This imposed a limitation on compatibility and universal usability of the coaxial cable. This meant that different coaxial cables could not be mixed when setting up a network, and it was very important to use the specified cable for the network being built.

Let's move on to discussing **cable plants**. A 'Cable Plant' is a term used to describe the complete installation of the network cable in the designated building. When we talk about a network's cable plant, we are referring to the network cables, the connectors, the wall plates, the patch panels, and the networking equipment related to networking cables installed in the building. On the surface, the network cable installation and cable management might seem like a simple to-do task, but quite the opposite. Cable plants are very difficult and complex; due to this, it is always recommended to choose a vendor that is adept and experienced in cable plant installation.

# Workstation Hardware

In a professional setting, the computers being used by the people connected on a network are network workstations. Generally, the workstations are the network client PCs on a network. However, workstations can also be modified to function as network servers. A workstation termed a 'network client' usually has these features.

1. It is an Intel-based computer

2. It is usually running a Microsoft Windows-based operating system

3. The install Operating System includes NIC and network client software (this enables the network client workstation to communicate with the network)

In the features mentioned above, we said that a network client workstation usually runs a version of Windows as the main OS. But the keyword here is 'usually.' There are cases where network workstations use an operating system other than Windows. Such computers have the hardware and software to allow the workstation to participate on the network even if the operating system is different. For example, Apple's Macintosh and Unix-based computers can also be used as network workstations.

# Utilizing the Network Traffic and Knowing the Network Hardware

In the earlier sections of this chapter, we discussed the hardware components involved in every network setup. We also learned about the purpose of each component in a network. In this section, we will go a step further and discuss the actual functionality of the hardware in directing network traffic.

In any network design, the very fundamental and basic approach to test its capability is to see how effectively the network can direct the network traffic from node to node. This test determines if the designed network is good enough or if it is underperforming. To perform this test, the first requirement is to put the network hardware components in a configuration that allows the network to send signals through the connected hardware components efficiently. This is done while keeping the type and connectivity pre-requisites of the network under consideration.

In this section, we will discuss the following basic networking hardware components.

- **Repeaters**: These devices lengthen the traveling distance of the network traffic in the corresponding network type.
- **Hubs** or **Concentrators**: These devices are used when setting up a network with a star topology. Hubs connect the different nodes.
- **Bridges**: These devices are the same as repeaters but more intelligent. Bridges direct network traffic to different segments. This is done so the segmentation is only performed if the traffic's destination is actually the other segment itself.
- **Routers**: These devices simply route the network traffic effectively and efficiently.
- **Switches**: These devices serve as a quick and efficient point-to-point connection for the other connected network hardware.

# Repeaters

A hardware device used in a network to lengthen the range of the network is called a repeater. Repeaters extend the network's reach by boosting the signals. Whenever a network is installed, it is a given there will be places where the network signal is weak. The repeater will take this network's side where the signal is weak, boost this weak signal, and then send it out through the other side. Repeaters are most commonly used for networks with a limited range, such as thin Ethernet networks. Hence you will see the use of repeaters in such network setups. However, this does not mean that using repeaters is limited.

But repeaters can be used for virtually any network connection. For example, consider a typical 100Base-T network installed using Cat-5 network cables. The maximum length of this cable is one hundred meters, meaning that's the range of the network. By using a repeater in this network setup, we can double the range of the network signal to two hundred meters.

In terms of the OSI networking model, operating repeaters is a process in the first layer, i.e., the physical layer. A repeater device is not intelligent. This means that a repeater does not have the hardware capability to understand the signals it is transmitting. Since the only job of the repeater is to perform a network signal amplification it needs to be used carefully. A repeater will not discern between a network signal and an interference signal (usually called "noise"). This is why they should be used only after careful assessment of the network. Otherwise, a repeater might amplify the noise in the network.

Repeaters cannot be used to connect different network mediums. For instance, if a repeater is being used with a 10Base-2 Thin Ethernet network, then it can be connected only with another 10Base-2 Thin Ethernet network.

If we critically analyze the intelligence of a repeater, then we can find it does possess a slight hint of intelligent functionality; nevertheless, this is not enough to perform complex operations such as discerning between the signal types being transmitted. The extent of the intelligent functionality of a repeater device is the ability to separate a connection from the others when the device detects any problem or anomaly in the connected network. For instance, let's consider that we are dealing with two segments of a thin ethernet network. These two segments are connected by a repeater device. If these two segments become broken, then instead of shutting down the entire network, the repeater will still allow the functional segment to keep on working. In this way, the users of the network can access the resources on the network segment still functional but won't have access to the resources on the broken segment. However, one thing to note here is that even if the repeater does separate the working segment from the broken segment, if the main resources such as the servers are on the broken segment, it will be useless. This is because even if the workstations were on the functional segment, they won't be able to access the main networking resources of the server.

The figure shown below depicts a typical repeater setup extending the length of the network.

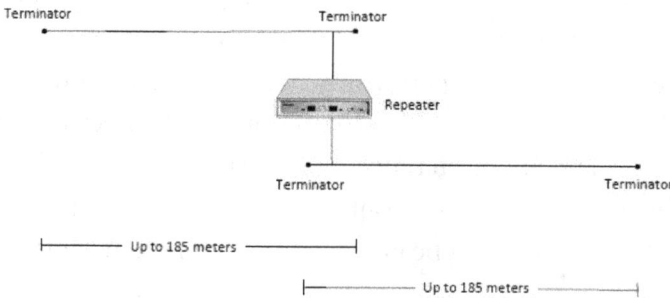

## Hubs (Concentrators)

Hubs are known by these terms:

- Intelligent LAN concentrators
- Concentrators

This hardware device is used in a network setup to connect the nodes to the backbones. If we discuss the topology of the network where hubs are being used, we can see that the nodes are connected to the hub in a star-like shape. This means that the network cables connected to the hub fan out to each corresponding node. This arrangement of the cables remains the same, whether a hub is being used in a star topology or a ring topology network. In smaller networks, there is no need for backbone switches, and hence, there is no need for a hub. However, hubs can be used in simple networks and large complex networks.

Regarding the compatibility of hubs with the network media types, fortunately, they offer seamless compatibility. This means that a hub can be used with any network without worrying about compatibility issues. If we go further and look at the top shelf higher-end models of hubs, we will see they feature a replaceable module through which a single hub can support multiple network media types. For example, a high-end hub model can support both Ethernet and Token-ring network modules.

Hubs come in many sizes. Some hubs offer support for up to 2 workstations while others for more than a hundred workstations. It all depends on the needs of the network.

Here are a few important characteristics of a hub.

- Just as how a sound from one source echoes in the farther depths of a cave, a hub echoes the data from each of its ports to all the other corresponding ports. Even though the wired arrangement of hubs is star-styled, their logical functioning is more akin to that of bus topology. However, due to the echoing of the data, no logic or filtering process can stop data packet collisions originating from the connected nodes.

- A distinguishing feature of hubs is that they can effectively cut off a misbehaving node from the other properly functioning nodes by shutting it off. This process is also known as 'partitioning.' The scenarios in which a hub partitions a node include detection of a network-cable short circuit, an excessive influx of data packets from a hub port flooding the network, and detection of a serious problem relating to the hub port. Effective partitioning of a malfunctioning node prevents the same effects from negatively affecting the other nodes functioning normally.

As technology is developing, the mechanics and infrastructure of a hub device are also becoming increasingly sophisticated. Newer versions and models of hubs include pretty neat and advanced features out of the box.

- Hubs now include a built-in management feature; by using network management protocols such as SNMP, a hub can be managed centrally, over the network.
- There are hubs now available that can automatically detect the connection speed of the network and run each node at that speed. For instance, a hub detecting a 10Base-T network will run each node at 10 Mbps. Similarly, for a 100Base-T network, the hub will run each node at 100 Mbps.
- Hubs are using uplinks with faster speeds to connect to a backbone. The average speed of the uplink is usually ten times that of the basic speed of the hub. For instance, a hub with a basic speed of 100 Mbps will have an uplink with a speed of 1 Gbps.
- Hubs now come with a built-in bridging and routing feature. Previously, networks using hubs would require separate dedicated hardware devices to perform bridging and routing functions. With this function built into the hubs, using such devices has become obsolete.
- Hubs feature a built-in switching function. With this feature, the hub can switch the nodes instead of sharing them.

When choosing a suitable hub for your network, the first thing to bear in mind is the specifications of your network. By knowing how many nodes are supposed to be connected to the hub, the required bandwidth for each node, and the network backbone type being used with the hub, we can choose the right hub best suited for the network. In terms of the network backbones usually installed with a hub, they are generally anything between shared 10 Mbps thin ethernet networks to 100 Mbps 100Base-Tx and high-speed networks. Whatever the case, the choosing of a backbone technology primarily depends on the bandwidth requirement of the network and other criteria that need to be fulfilled for the network designed.

Technically, in a network where hubs are being used, the hubs act as 'collision domains', where collisions usually occur. So, if we use multiple hubs in a single network set up, then the area of the collision domain in the network will inevitably become larger. The only exception is when the hubs are individually connected to a switch. By using switches, we can restrict the collision domains of each hub to itself. The figure shown below depicts a network using several hubs.

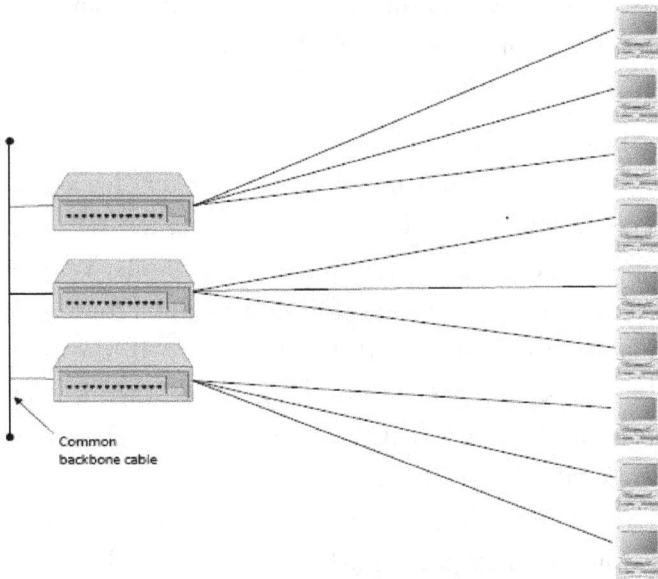

Common
backbone cable

# Switches

Just as the name implies, a switch is a hardware component of a network that can rapidly switch connections from port to port. A switch creates these connections in a network by switching dynamically among the several network ports available. Consider a train yard, where several trains are coming in from certain tracks and leaving through other tracks. The train yard has a designated person tasked to manage the movement and routes of the train. This person is called the 'yard manager.' To make sure that the trains arrive at their destination, the yard manager essentially switches the tracks according to their specified route. In this analogy, the 'switch' is the 'yard manager.' Instead of directing trains by switching the tracks, a switch directs the data packets through the network by ethernet cabling. In this way, a data packet is effectively routed to its destination.

We know that a switch establishes an individualized connection between any two given ports of the network; it makes sense that the entire ports converging into the switch device don't share a common collision domain. This is why a switch device plays a role somewhat similar to that of a super bridge.

Due to the nature of switches, they are mostly used to bridge the connection between hubs and relatively faster backbones in a network. For instance, consider a network using ten hubs. Each hub supports up to 24 connection nodes for workstations. With ten hubs, we will have about 240 connection nodes meaning there will be 240 workstations in total connected to the hubs. If these hubs are connected to the same backbone in the network, then it would mean that the collision domain of all the hubs would be the same. When the 240 workstations are sharing the same collision domain, then network performance will deteriorate. Here, we can fix this problem by using a switch with 12 ports. Earlier, each port of the switch had its own separate collision domain. Here, all ten of the hubs connected to the 12-port switch will have domains, thereby maintaining the network quality.

A 100Base-T network connection is commonly used with workstations. A networking expert would recommend a 1000Base-T or faster connection as the backbone network. By using a switch and a fast backbone, the workstations connected to the network through the nodes can operate at 100 Mbps.

Switches impact the speed and performance of the network so well that using a switch becomes a no-brainer. Another aspect that makes switches so desirable in networks is that they are very inexpensive. For a typical local area network, using switches instead of hubs makes more sense because hubs are expensive network components. In comparison, a switch is inexpensive, has much to offer to the network, and is comparatively easier and simple to install. Nowadays, you might find difficulty finding an available bridge on the market as the supply and demand of switches is overwhelming.

The reason to know and understand hubs is that although they are not used now, you might still come across older installations using hubs. In newer network installations, it is guaranteed that you will exclusively deal with switches instead. To reiterate the main concept of these hubs and switches, hubs create a bigger packet collision domain, while switches have smaller, separated collision domains.

# Bridges

A bridge is a hardware device that performs the same function as a repeater but is more intelligent. Bridges work by joining two network segments, just like repeaters; the main difference is that when a bridge must pass data traffic from a segment to another segment, it does so intelligently. This means that a bridge will only pass the data traffic to the other segment if this traffic's destination is the target segment; otherwise, it will not. Another distinguishing feature of a bridge is that they also divide the network into smaller segments. Certain bridges can be connected to two network segments. For instance, such a bridge can span from coaxial Thin Ethernet to a twisted-pair Token Ring.

We talked about the layer at which repeaters operate at (which was the physical layer of the OSI model). One would assume that since the function and purpose of the bridges is virtually the same as repeaters, they would also operate at the first layer of the OSI networking model. However, that's not the case; instead, the bridges operate at a layer that is one level higher, i.e., at the second layer, also known as the data-link layer in the OSI networking model. This is because bridges connect the network segments and then pass the data traffic from segment to the other segment 'intelligently.' To do this, the bridge analyzes each encountered data packet's MAC, or Media Access Control address. This analysis of the MAC address helps the bridge determine whether it should forward the data packet onto the other network or not. A bridge device can store the parts of the network's address data. This can be done in either of two ways.

1. The user programs a static routing table that contains the address information and data.

2. The user implements a dynamic learning system that learns in a tree pattern by automatically identifying and discovering the network's addresses.

Bridges shouldn't be used carelessly. Here are scenarios where using bridges in the network is recommended.

- If you are dealing with a small-scale network, then bridges can be used.

- If the network is using a repeater, then a bridge can be installed in place of the repeater.

- If the network you are dealing with seems to benefit when the network traffic is not transferred unnecessarily between the different segments of a network, then a bridge should be used.

# Routers

Continuing the chain of intelligent iterations of the other hardware components of a network, a router is basically a bridge, but even more intelligent, just as a bridge is an intelligent version of a repeater. Just as bridges operate at one layer higher (at the data-link layer) in the OSI networking model than repeaters, routers operate at the third layer of the OSI networking model, also known as the network layer. Routers are more efficient and far better than bridges for transmitting data packets to their respective destinations.

Since the operation of the router is at the third layer of the OSI networking model, the only requirement for the upper layers of the OSI model to establish a connection with the router is that of using the same protocols. If the router is configured and designed specifically for protocol translation, then it can translate any protocol from the first three layers (physical, datalink and network layers) to any other protocol also a part of these three layers. A router can also connect two networks that have no similarity to each other (while connecting similar networks is a given). Generally, routers are best suited and commonly used for Wide Area Networks (WAN) as they can effectively create the links required for this network to be established.

If we analyze the characteristics of the router which allow it to effectively connect two similar or dissimilar networks, we conclude that a router essentially serves the purpose of a node. Routers feature their very own network address, which solidifies their function as a node even more. A router receives data packets from other nodes. After receiving the packets, the router analyzes and examines the contents of the data packets: only after this assessment does the router send the data packet to its destination. This procedure needs to be performed almost instantaneously to avoid delay and lag in data traffic. To ensure that the router swiftly and accurately performs this job, they are designed with a microprocessor inside them to handle the computational and logical needs of the task. Usually, this processor is a variant of the RISC or Reduced Instruction Set Computer type chip. Besides a microprocessor, routers also have built-in memory to help with routing function. Since routers are more intelligent than bridges and they have more computational resources;

they can figure out the shortest route (if available) towards any data packet's destination and use it.

Besides this, routers can also perform certain tasks that facilitate the bandwidth maximization of a network. Also, a router can logically and dynamically adapt to the traffic problems detected in a network.

Let's talk about the importance of routers in a network. It wouldn't be an exaggeration to say that routers form the backbone of the entire Internet. For instance, consider the TRACERT command. When you use this command to trace a route from two points, a node to a destination, we can see there are multiple 'hops' shown by the terminal before it can show the destination. These 'hops' are routers that are forwarding the data packet until it reaches its destination.

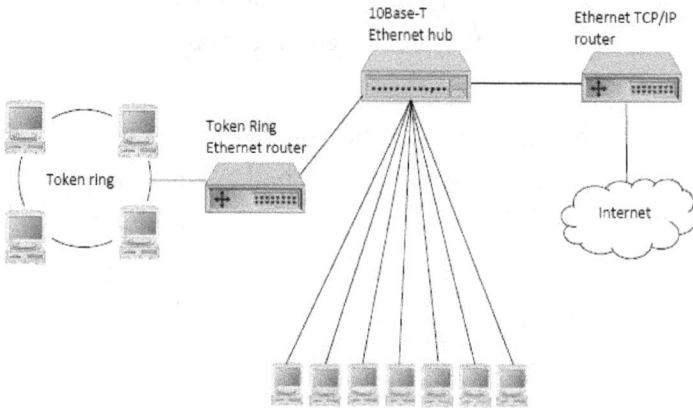

Routers are not pre-configured. To perform their tasks and functions properly, they need to be programmed. For instance, a standard router configuration may include the assignment of network addresses to each of its ports and the configuration of the protocol settings. The programming of routers is usually done in either of these two ways.

1. Usually, there is a port known as the 'RS-232C' port. By using terminal emulation software, we can connect a computer or

a terminal using this port. Once connected, it becomes possible to program the router in text mode.

2. Besides programming a router directly from its RS-232C port, routers can also be programmed by using network-based software that comes with it. Usually, this software uses either a graphical tool or a simple web interface.

Both of these two methods are supported by the majority of the routers available nowadays. However, there is no recommended method. It all depends on aspects such as your security needs and the specific model of the router you are using. When using routers, one should be careful, as the network-based programming method for a router can be exploited by hackers. This would allow unauthorized users to change the configuration of the router.

# Gateways

A gateway is an application-specific interface. The main job of a gateway is to link all layers of the OSI networking model whenever they are detected to be dissimilar. This dissimilarity can be in any single layer or all layers and the gateway will still perform its function. To understand this better, let's see an example. Let's say we have established networks by using the OSI networking model, but we want to connect to a network using Systems Network Architecture, also known as SNA, by IBM. These two networks are not similar, so to connect them, we will use a gateway to do so. Gateways also can translate Ethernet to Token Ring. However, there are simpler network solutions if you need a network translation such as this one. Since the translation load on gateways is considerably larger than other solutions, gateways perform relatively slower.

Nowadays, using gateways in networking is primarily to handle e-mails. For example, two of the most common e-mail protocols handled by gateways are:

- POP3
- SMTP

Generally, the majority of the e-mail systems that need to connect with systems on a different network will either use a computer set up as a gateway or use the e-mail server to perform the gateway tasks.

# The Core Fundamentals of Cable Topologies

Before we move on to the cable topologies, let's refresh the concept of a 'Topology.' The word 'Topology' means 'shape'; similarly, the word 'Network Topology' essentially refers to a network's shape (the wired arrangement of the network's nodes).

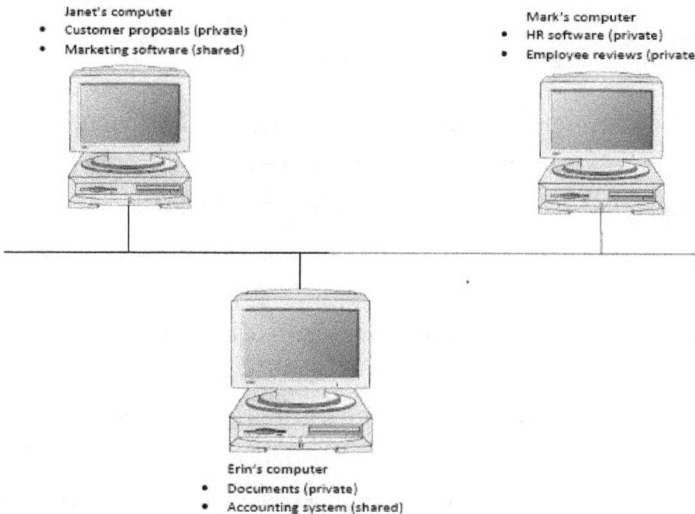

Janet's computer
- Customer proposals (private)
- Marketing software (shared)

Mark's computer
- HR software (private)
- Employee reviews (private)

Erin's computer
- Documents (private)
- Accounting system (shared)

Different topologies have different costs, advantages, disadvantages, performance, stability, and reliability. In this section, we will discuss the three main cable topologies commonly used today.

1. Bus Topology
2. Star Topology
3. Ring Topology
4.

## Bus Topology

Bus topology is also commonly called 'Common bus multipoint topology.' A bus topology is basically a network that uses a single end-to-end network cable. On this network cable, some devices are connected at different locations on the cable, and these connections are termed 'nodes.' A simple illustration of a bus topology network is shown below:

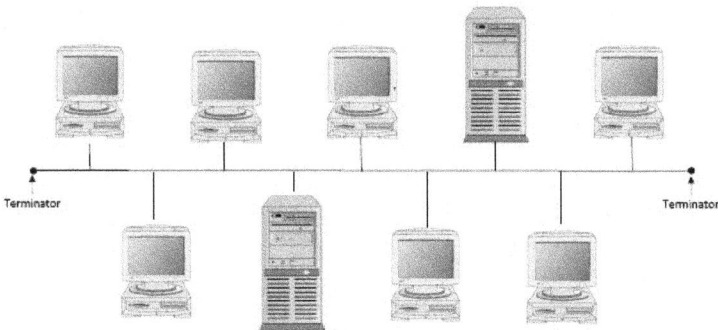

However, there is no universal bus topology in use. Instead, bus topology comes in many types, each featuring its own specifications. These specifications are based on these factors:

- The number of nodes that can be handled by a single segment
- By using a repeater, what is the resulting number of segments that can be used
- The maximum limit of physical proximity for the nodes
- The network segment's length
- The coaxial cable required
- How the segment's terminal ends are supposed to be terminated

Generally, a bus topology network implements coaxial cable. In such a type of network, the two open terminal ends of the network need to be addressed; otherwise, the network would not be functional. A special type of cable terminator is used on each terminal end of the network.

There are several different bus topology, and each group uses a different type of connector to conjoin the different segments of the network cable. For instance, a Thin Ethernet 10Base-2 bus topology network uses a connector known as a 'BNC connector.' This connector is also known as the 'BNC-T connector' because it resembles a 'T' shape. This connector allows a node (computer or a server) to be connected to the network segment while allowing the network to continue its bus. There are also different types of BNC connectors:

1. BNC-T connector
2. BNC barrel connector
3. RG-58 cable with male BNC connector

In terms of budget, the bus topology network is the least expensive option of the three. This is because a bus topology network uses comparatively less network cable regarding the star and ring topology. Hence, a bus topology network uses less networking materials and needs less installation labor. However, while the bus topology has advantages over the other two topologies with cost, it also has significant drawbacks.

A network with a bus topology is more sensitive and prone to failure because it comprises multiple subscales, which essentially create a segment. These subscales must be connected to the nodes. Now, this level of intricacy introduces a new problem, and that is:

- If the segments of the bus topology network fail, it will cause the failure of the segments in the network.
- Identifying the source of failure is even more tedious and time-consuming, as the technician must go through the

available cable connections until the source of the defective segment is identified.

Since a bus topology network is seemingly unreliable and more prone to failure, many new wired network installations do not use this topology. However, bus topology networks may be seen in older network installations.

The most commonly used bus topology network used back in the day and still in limited existence today is the 10Base-2 Ethernet network (also known as Thin Ethernet). A Thin Ethernet network has these characteristics:

- 10 Mbps maximum speed rating
- Type of network cable and connectors used are '**RG-58/AU**' or '**RG-58/CU**' (coaxial cable and BNC connectors respectively)
- To function properly, the network requires each ending of every segment to be terminated with a 50-ohm terminating connector
- Maximum node capacity per segment is 30 nodes
- Maximum segment length is 185 meters, or 607 feet
- Repeaters can feature extended segments
- The minimum distance between each node should be 0.5 meters or 1.5 feet of cable distance.

In a network using bus topology, with repeaters enabling the user to connect up to three segments together, each connected segment would support up to 30 nodes (counting the repeater as a node). Two more segments could be added, if the sole purpose was extended signal distance and they had no nodes connected to them. This would make five segments that could be added by using a repeater. The maximum length of the entire repeated segment should not exceed 925 meters, or 3,035 feet. To remember this arrangement, we can simply remember the 5-4-3 rule:

- Five segments
- Four repeaters
- Three populated segments

# Star Topology

In a star topology network, the connected computers, servers, or simply nodes are hooked up to a single central unit. In this wired arrangement, the connections radiate out from the main unit, similar to the shape of a star. This central unit is commonly called a 'hub' or 'concentrator.' The hub hosts a bunch of network cables that radiate out to the corresponding nodes on the network. In technical terms, a hub is known as a 'Multistation Access Unit' or simply 'MAU.' However, this term is strictly used with Token Ring networks.

In a star topology network, there are multiple hub size options available. For instance, some hubs can support no more than two nodes, while there are also hubs that can support up to ninety-six nodes. Generally, a standard central hub unit used in this network has support for up to 24 nodes. Regardless, even if we use a 24-node hub or a 96-node hub, we are still given the freedom of connecting multiple nodes into a hub and shaping the network as we see fit. Here's a simple illustration of a star topology network.

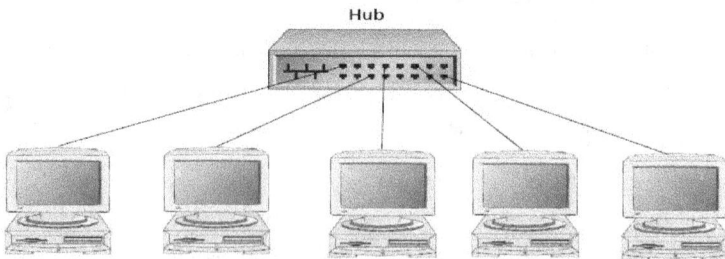

However, remember that, since a hub is used as the central unit, there come complications in the previous sections of this chapter. A hub echoes the network traffic among its other ports. So, the network traffic from any node will be echoed to the other nodes. This means that a node's entire bandwidth connection is shared among the other node connections. For instance, if the total bandwidth speed of the hub is 100 Mbps, but one nod is using only 50 Mbps of that total bandwidth, then the other nodes cannot access the rest of the bandwidth and instead, must share this 50 Mbps. To put it into simpler terms, the total bandwidth available to one node is the same bandwidth shared among the other nodes.

In a star topology network, there are multiple Ethernet connections available for use listed below.

- **100Base-T Ethernet** is the most commonly used and provides a bandwidth limit of up to 100 Mbps.
- **10Base-T Ethernet** is seen in older networks. This ethernet has a bandwidth limit of up to 10 Mbps
- **1000Base-T Ethernet** is a relatively newer Ethernet standard and is commonly known as Gigabit Ethernet. It offers a bandwidth capacity of 1000 Mbps or 1 Gbps.
- **10GBase-X** is the most recent Ethernet standard. It is called 10 Gigabit Ethernet and uses a fiber optic cable connection offering a bandwidth capacity of 10 Gbps.

Let's talk about the cable requirements of the 10Base-T and 100Base-T Ethernet network connections.

- 10Base-T Ethernet requires a Category 3 (Cat-3) twisted-pair network cable.
- 100Base-T Ethernet requires a Category 5 (Cat-5) twisted-pair network cable.

Remember that although 10Base-T Ethernet can use a Cat-5 network cable, 100Base-T Ethernet cannot use Cat-3 network cables. Whenever installing a 10Base-T Ethernet or newer network connections, it is recommended to use the latest networking cables. For instance, if you are using a 10Base-T Ethernet connection, then you can use a Cat-5E, and if money is not a problem, then you can even go for the Cat-6 network cable.

Here are wiring characteristics that 10Base-T networks share.

- They require four wires in two single-sheathed twisted pairs. These twisted pair wires can either be shielded or unshielded.
- They can function on Cat-3 network cables and newer ones such as Cat-5.
- There is a length limit for each node connection of 100 meters, or roughly 328 feet.
- They are not bound by a limitation on the number of nodes per logical segment.
- For all of their connections, they use 'RJ-45' connectors.

A notable advantage that 1000Base-T networks have over 100Base-T networks is that they:

- Are compatible with Cat-5 network cables
- Operate at ten times the speed of 100Base-T networks, i.e., at 1 Gbps or 1000 Mbps as opposed to 100 Mbps

Arguably one of the most important advantages that 1000Base-T networks have is their Cat-5 cable compatibility. Nowadays, the most commonly used network cable in over 75% of the installed networks is none other than Cat-5 cables. If a Cat-5 cable system is already present, a 1000Base-T network can be installed without changing the cable system. This provides a huge saving in not only time but in installation costs, cabling costs, and labor costs, since installing a new cable networking standard for a whole building is very expensive.

Here are a few characteristics of 1000Base-T over Cat-5 networks.

- These networks need eight wires in four single-sheathed twisted pairs.
- They require at least Cat-5 or better network cable standards (Cat-5E or Cat-6).

- The length limit for each node connection is 100 meters or roughly 328 feet.
- They are not bound by a limitation on the number of nodes per logical segment.
- For all of their connections, they use 'RJ-45' connectors.

You will see that 1000Base-T networks are strikingly similar to their predecessor 100Base-T networks except in areas such as network cabling requirements.

Star topology networks are more expensive than bus topology networks because the use of wired network cables is greater. Also, the labor costs to install that wire is more expensive, and the need for routers or hubs also stacks up the overall cost. However, this expensive budget is not worthless. Star topologies are more reliable and offer better performance than networks using a bus topology. Not only does it offer higher bandwidth performance, if the isolated network connections break or go bad, but the other connections will remain unaffected. Even if a problem does come up in a star topology network, it is easy and simple to troubleshoot as each network cable is going from the hub to the node directly.

# Ring Topology

Unlike the other two topologies we have discussed so far, that use an arrangement of physical network cables, a ring topology network uses a logical arrangement instead. To elaborate, in a ring topology the actual physical network cable arrangement is that of a star topology, and each node of the cable is connected to their very own Media Access Units. But here's the catch; despite the physical arrangement, the network cables electrically behave as a ring. This means that the signals coming from the network travel through the different nodes in a ring. A simple illustration of a ring topology network is shown below.

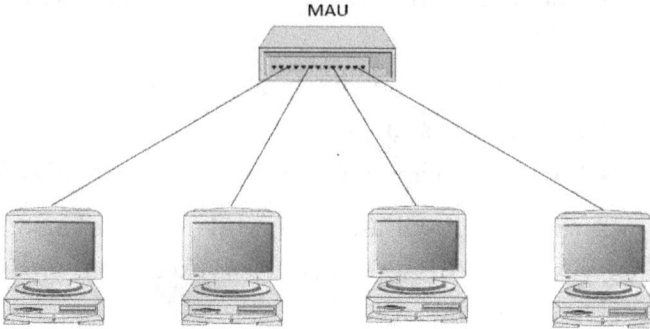

(Physical Representation of Ring Topology)

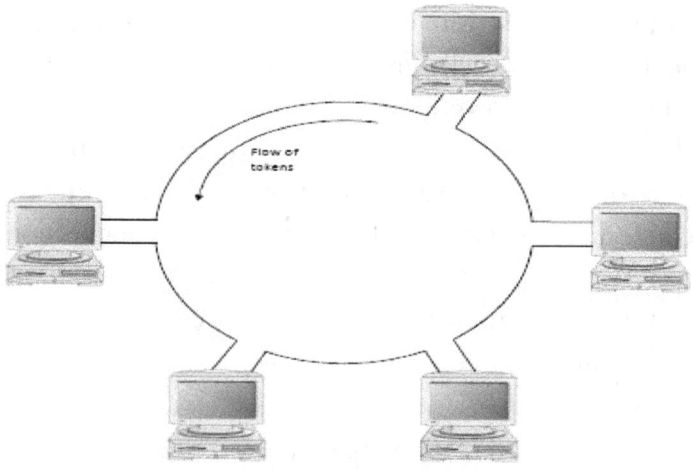

Flow of
tokens

(Electrical Representation of a Ring Topology)

Unlike the bus and star network topologies based on Ethernet, the ring topology is based on Token Rings instead. Sometimes, a network using a ring topology can also be seen running on a fiber-optic network, usually with a bandwidth capacity of 100 Mbps instead of copper-based cables. This network is based on FDDI or Fiber Distributed Data Interface. The main use of a ring topology is for big telecommunication networks such as the Synchronous Optical Network, which is also known as SONET. Ring topology is also used in storage area networks.

# Chapter 4: Wireless Communication Systems and Connecting to the Internet

## What is Wireless Communication?

Wireless communication rarely requires a physical medium or a channel to transmit the signals. Rather these allow the signals to travel through space and are commonly called an unguided medium of communication.

## Connecting to the Internet

In this section, you will learn about the fundamentals of Internet connectivity and its features.

## Wide Area Networks

Wide Area Networks or WAN is just a Local Area Network with a wider range. Wide Area Networks can be defined as multiple interconnected Local Area Networks. WANs are preferred when a better and wider range approach is required of a Local Area Network. Establishing Wide Area Networks can be done in multiple ways. To determine which method to adopt in setting up a WAN, the organization or company need to consider different aspects such as

- The regularity with which the Local Area Networks must be used.
- The regularity with which the Local Area Networks must be connected with each other.
- The "bandwidth", or data capacity required by the network.
- The measurement of the distance between each Local Area Network point.

By factoring in these aspects, a suitable solution can be implemented to establish an optimal Wide Area Network. For instance:

1. Establishing a Wide Area Network using a leased telephone line capable of supporting a bandwidth of up to 56Kbps.
2. Establishing a Wide Area Network using dedicated DS1 lines capable of supporting a bandwidth of up to 1.544 Mbps.
3. Establishing a Wide Area Network using dedicated DS3 lines capable of supporting a bandwidth of up to 44.736 Mbps.

A Wide Area Network can even be established by using a private satellite, which ultimately supports even higher bandwidth. Hence, to choose the best option for a WAN connection, it is recommended first to assess the situation and needs to come to a clear solution.

The emergence of Wide Area Networks began when users on a Local Area Network needed to access the resources on another Local Area Network. This was all too often observed in big institutions such as business companies, organizations, hospitals, banks, and schools, etc.

Let's discuss a brief example. Consider a big company with several buildings specializing in their respective functions. There's the main headquarters of the company, and then there are the warehouse units of the same company but in a different location. Now, the main headquarters of the company houses some much-needed resources such as the ERP, or Enterprise Resource Planning system. For the warehouse to properly perform its job, it needs access to the inventory and shipping functions provided by this resource. Since the warehouse and the headquarters are in different physical locations, the Local Area Network of the warehouse needs access to the Local Area Network of the headquarter. So, the company will implement a Wide Area Network connection to resolve this issue.

Generally, if an organization can design the infrastructure of its system so it does not need a Wide Area Network connection, this is better. The reason for this lies in the cost required to maintain the Wide Area Network links properly.

# Internet and Intranet

Remembering the wide-spread popularity of the Internet and its importance in our modern society, the productivity of any business company is crippled if they do not properly use the Internet. Handling and maintaining Internet connectivity on a network is a very pivotal job, as even several minutes of Internet downtime can create a pile of problems for the organization. Hence, the Internet is a very crucial service and feature of computer networking. Now, very few people are unfamiliar with the Internet. With its amazing productivity and reachability, virtually all companies today take advantage of the Internet's key services such as e-mails, accessing the World Wide Web, and using the Usenet newsgroups.

Implementing an Internet connection on a network involves another entity known as the Internet Service Provider (ISP). The connection of a person or organization with the ISP is basically a telecommunications network connection. The connection from the ISP to the client is established by using a physical medium such as a line. There are several types of connections offered by ISPs depending on the client, for example

- DSL line
- ISDN line
- Fractional/Full DS1 connection

After a suitable line supported by the ISP is chosen, it is installed into the designated domicile by stretching the line to the building and connecting it to a special box, which is known as a CSU/DSU (channel service unit and data service unit). The main purpose of this box is data conversion, i.e., converting the form of data being carried by the specified local telephone company into a form usable by the Local Area Network. Also, this CSU/DSU box is then connected to a router (or a modem), which handles the routing of data packets between the Local Area Network and the Internet. Sometimes, this CSU/DSU box is built within the router provided by the ISP.

Now let's discuss the security of an Internet connection. When an ISP "ships" an Internet connection to its client, they provide them with a router during the installation. The data packets being sent out by this router are automatically filtered to prevent a data packet leak.

The more common software-based security generally adopted by users is a 'firewall.' This program is what intelligently limits any unnecessary connection to a server on the Internet that an application on the computer might request. It also blocks harmful incoming traffic, which is usually from a hacker. So, by using a firewall, we can secure our computer systems from potential online threats while using the Internet.

So far, we have discussed the Internet as an immensely interconnected network of people around the world. We will now discuss something similar to the Internet, and that is the 'Intranet.' They sound and work similarly.

While the Internet is basically focused on external connectivity, an intranet is a form of network focused on internal connectivity. For instance, let's say there is a company that wants to host a web page or even a server only for its employees to access. It needs an Intranet. The company will use a primary web server that will store all the resources of the company, such as documents, employee handbooks, invoices, and all such data regularly published within the company for the employees and departments. Hence, it becomes a miniaturized version of the Internet solely dedicated to the internal network infrastructure of the organization. However, the functionality of the intranet does not simply end here. It can perform Internet-related tasks, such as providing File Transfer Protocol (FTP) and Usenet servers.

An intranet is implemented and maintained by the organization or company within the limits of its own Local Area Network. Usually, an intranet is not accessible from outside the LAN, but there are cases where penetration can happen.

## Understanding the Features of Networking

Up to now, we have discussed the simple relationship between computers connected on a network (P2P and Client-Server Networks). Now that the reader has developed an understanding of how connected computers interact with each other, we can discuss some tasks that they can perform on a network. This can be called the features of computer networking. In this section we will discuss these features:

- File Sharing
- Printer Sharing
- Application Services
- E-mail
- Remote Access

# File Sharing

Back in the day, file sharing was the very reason that people would use computer networks. In the mid-1980s the ability to share files and data from one computer to the other connected in a network without using physical storage devices was a revolutionary deal. Although it may not seem like much today, consider this: to share a file or media content with your acquaintance, you first had to store it in removable media storage and then physically get that media to that person. File sharing was so important that companies would specifically install a computer network to use this feature.

File sharing usually entails the files that people would need to access regularly. Spreadsheets and word processing files are common examples, although there are many others. To enable file sharing, the first requirement is for those computers that require shared access to be connected in a network. Next, there should be a 'shared drive' which acts as a network place for the files to be stored while allowing users connected to the same network to access these shared files on their system remotely. To eliminate a repercussion of file sharing, namely that any user can modify the contents of the shared file, the system should have proper authorization privileges in place. This means that not every user in a computer network will have administrator rights that will allow them to change the files or the shared drive. This is also known as 'file locking.' Another reason for file locking is so the multiple users who are accessing the shared drive or the folder are not modifying it with conflicting changes simultaneously.

# Printer Sharing

The printer sharing feature is also of great importance and makes computer networking even more useful. As the name suggests, printer sharing refers to sharing the printing resources between users within a computer network. If a company places a printer in one office, then it is possible to share the functionality of this single printer with every employee in the office using a computer network. This is not only economical for the company but the users. Since the office requires only one printer, the company can afford to pitch in for some high-quality top of the line printer designed to handle huge workloads. By implementing a computer network, a company can enjoy the economic benefits of printer sharing.

Now we'll discuss some details of how printer sharing works. Even though there are multiple ways printer sharing can be done, the most common method is to use a printing queue that holds the printing requests of the users in the interconnected computer network. This queue ensures that the printing task in progress is not disturbed by the other incoming printing requests, and the new printing tasks are not performed by the machine until the current task is completed. This method is recommended due to its efficiency.

Another way of performing printer sharing is to allow the independent workstations to have direct access to the printer itself. The printer itself supports a setting where it's configured to connect to a network as an ordinary workstation would. If there is a high demand for the resources of the shared printer, then the independent workstations are instructed to stand-by until it's their respective turn. But this is not efficient.

In the printer queue method, there is a special server known as the 'print server' which automates sending print requests according to their timestamps or urgency. There are several ways to set up a print server.

1. Using a file server connected to the printer network.

2. Using a workstation running special printing software and is connected to the network and printer. In this way, the software communicates with the other computers on the network, taking their print requests and forwarding them to the printer through the host computer.

# Application Services

This feature is similar to the two features we have recently explored, i.e., file sharing and printer sharing. The application service feature allows users connected on a network to share applications. For instance, if a company invests in a licensed software to be used by its employees, then it can take advantage of computer networking to generate shared copies of the application on to the network server to be used by others. The working of this feature is very simple; a workstation connected to a network can access the shared application, load the files from the shared drive into its system memory, and run the program.

By using this feature, the organization can also save on effective storage on its workstations, as every user would access a centralized folder on a server to run a program instead of installing the same program individually on each running workstation.

Another way to use this feature is to establish a shared installation point on a network server. This allows the users who wish to install the application to access the installation setup directly from the network instead of downloading it or using physical media storage such as CDs, DVDs, etc. Hence, the user can directly copy the contents of the installation setup for the program onto their respective workstations and install the program as usual.

# E-mail

It wouldn't be an exaggeration to regard e-mail as one of the most resourceful, convenient, and efficient ways of communication that have ever emerged. The e-mail feature observes a widespread use in different environments, be it a local or professional setting. On the outside, e-mail seems very simple with a sender and receiver. Although this covers the gist of it, we will explore the e-mail feature in more technical terms.

Generally, there are two types of e-mail systems. One is a file-based e-mail system, while the other is a client-server-based e-mail system. The one most people are readily familiar with is the client-server-based e-mail system, but we will come to that later. First, we will discuss how a file-based e-mail system works.

A file-based e-mail system is simply made up of a server and a controlling host known as a 'gateway server.' The server defines a storage location that consists of shared files. The server is to provide authorized users access to these files. However, handling the connection requests between the server and an external user falls under the jurisdiction of the 'gateway server,' which is actually a single computer. This computer runs a special software known as 'gateway software' to handle this job, and the unity of the server and gateway server is what makes up a file-based e-mail system.

But a client-server-based e-mail system is something cleaner, sleeker, more powerful, and, most important, secure. This e-mail system also boasts extended functionality; for instance, in business companies, they can automate the e-mail system for generating invoices and making purchases automatically. It's a given that such an e-mail system must be properly configured to do so. The client-server-based e-mail system consists of a single server responsible for collectively managing the external and internal e-mail interconnections on the network. This e-mail system also houses the messages. Some examples of a client-server-based e-mail system are Microsoft Exchange and Lotus Notes.

Until now, we have mainly discussed these two e-mail systems in large-scale business companies. However, the e-mail feature is equally important for small-scale companies and organizations, such as those with less than twenty-five employees. For such companies, purchasing an entire e-mail system and maintaining it is comparatively expensive and requires much manpower for proper maintenance, hence making the use of e-mail systems out of their reach. However, there is another viable alternative for such scenarios. This includes using an e-mail system not primarily housed and maintained within the organization itself. For instance:

- Set up a shared connection with the Internet so every employee using a workstation can access it. Next, we have to do only simply set up the corresponding e-mail accounts for the users either through the ISP or just use an e-mail service free and popular such as Yahoo!, Hotmail, Gmail, etc.

- Use the 'Microsoft Windows Small Business Server 2008' as the dedicated Operating System for all the workstations. This OS includes useful server-based tools that can facilitate setting up an e-mail system. Best of all, the OS is natively bundled with a limited version of the 'Exchange Server' software that can be used.

- Subscribe to a mailbox from a service provider that has set up and maintained an e-mail system with high specifications. Companies that go for this approach usually have just to pay a monthly fee that corresponds to the number of mailboxes being used by them.

# Remote Access

Another beneficial feature of computer networking is giving users the ability to remotely access the resources of their specific network. The reason that makes this feature so important is that a network's physical limitations are ignored by the users, meaning they don't need to be in the office or the building where the network is located. They can remotely access their files or e-mails even when they're working away from the office, such as in their homes or a hotel. However, remote access is not a simple feature. But remote access can be delivered in a variety of flavors. To set up and use the remote access feature, the list shown below outlines several methods that can serve the purpose.

• Using the Microsoft Windows Server operating system to establish a RAS (Remote Access Service) connection. This connection entails a simple setup consisting of only one modem to an enlarged system that involves multiple modems.

• Using a remote access system set up and maintained to perform only this function. Such a system can handle multiple simultaneous connections at once, meaning that several computers can be set up easily. Each computer that is connected to the remote access system uses its own network card.

• Setting up a workstation with specific remote access software (for example, pcAnywhere and GoToMyPC) through which the users that intend to use the remote access feature simply dial in.

• Establishing a company connection to the Internet. The employees of this company can use this Internet connection to gain access to the resources available on the company's networking system. To secure this remote access, the company usually implements a Virtual Private Network connection (VPN).

• Using a workstation running the Windows Server operating system as a connection server. This can be done by installing software such as Windows Terminal Services. In this way, the workstation will be capable of hosting several client sessions allowing multiple users to gain remote access.

# Chapter 5: Common Network Protocols and Ports

Unlike the previous chapter, which covered more than half the topics under the scope of this book, we will be briefly going over and understanding some of the most common protocols we come across in networks. Network protocols are complex and difficult. We will reserve the more intricate details for the next series of this book and focus instead on the fundamentals of network protocols to build a basic conceptual foundation.

In this chapter, we will be mainly discussing:

- TCP/IP and UDP Ports
- Other network protocols such as DNS, DHCP, HTTP, FTP, etc.

## TCP/IP and UDP

TCP and IP are two protocols used in harmony with each other. The explanation of each protocol is:

1. **TCP:** Also known as the 'Transmission Control Protocol.' TCP operates at the transport layer of the OSI model, and it mainly manages the connection between the

computers on a network. The messages of the TCP protocol are 'encapsulated' in IP datagrams.

2. **IP:** Also known as the 'Internet Protocol.' IP operates at the third layer of the OSI networking model, i.e., the network layer. The main function of this protocol is to define the way network data is supposed to be addressed from its source to destination, respectively. IP also defines the sequence in which the data is supposed to be reassembled when it reaches its destination.

UDP is known as 'User Datagram Protocol,' and it basically has the same job as TCP/IP protocols, with the only catch being that it offers limited features as compared to its counterparts. Although the UDP protocol is also carried by the IP datagrams, it has only a reliability feature, and that is that the UDP protocol will resend the data packets that did not arrive at the destination.

The only advantage UDP has over TCP/IP is that it is considerably faster. However, it offers little error-checking and correction capability. Hence, UDP is best suited for trivial network communication tasks. Since UDP does not check for errors and simply resends the data when any error does come up, it should be only used for network communication when the reliability features are not important or if the application involved in the network communication offers its own extensive error handling and checking.

The other networking protocols have been explained in chapter 2. Recall that they are:

Domain Name System (DNS), **allowing users to access websites with easy-to-remember domain names instead of long numerical IP addresses.**

Dynamic Host Configuration Protocol (DHCP), **for assigning TCP/IP addresses to the nodes in a network.**

Hypertext Transfer Protocol (HTTP), **which controls the transfer of data between the client and the webserver.**

File Transfer Protocol (FTP), which defines the method by which file data is sent and received between the FTP client and the FTP server.

Network News Transfer Protocol (NNTP), specifically used for Usenet discussion groups on the Internet.

Simple Mail Transfer Protocol (SMTP), which handles the sending and receiving of e-mails from one e-mail server to another.

# Chapter 6: Learning About the OSI Networking Model

The very important, fundamental key to understanding computer networking is to perceive the conceptual realms of the OSI networking model. This is where all the beginners in IT start. The OSI model defines most methods along with the protocols through which computers connect and communicate with each other on a network. When understanding the OSI networking model, the reader must firmly grasp the abstract visualizations as this will help create a strong foundation for network designing and network solution engineering.

The OSI model is an accurate yet fundamental portrait of how networking in the real world actually works. Although there are subtle differences between the theories and practical implementation of the networking, it is by no means something that one should disregard.

By understanding the OSI model, we are essentially learning about the intricacies of computer networking, and the reader can eventually visualize the networking process of computers. And this understanding is the key to success in the practical field of networking. The basis of a certified networking professional is to have an adept and comprehensive understanding of the OSI networking model itself.

We have discussed the importance of the OSI model enough, now let's talk about what it's all about. As the name suggests, the OSI Networking Model is simply a framework that defines the operations and workings of modern networks. The model is divided into seven distinct and separate layers. Each layer possesses a trait known as 'successive dependence.' This means that the successively higher layers in the model depend largely on the services characteristic of the preceding lower layers.

To understand this better, let's use an analogy. Think of a standard desktop computer system you would commonly find in your home. Now, this computer's several components work together, which makes the computer itself functional. If we divided this computer into layers such as in the OSI networking model, then according to this standard, the hardware component of this computer will be termed as the 'lowest layer.' The layer succeeding the 'hardware layer' of this computer would be the Operating System along with the respective system drivers. It's a no-brainer that the Operating System and the respective drivers would be useless without the corresponding hardware. Hence, this higher layer is depending on the preceding lower layer to perform its function properly. Similarly, this successive hierarchy extends to the point where an application is displaying useful and digestible data to the user.

The seven layers of the OSI Networking Model are:

8. Physical Layer
9. Data Link Layer
10. Network Layer
11. Transport Layer
12. Session Layer
13. Presentation Layer
14. Application Layer

The figure shown below depicts the structure of the OSI networking model in its basic form.

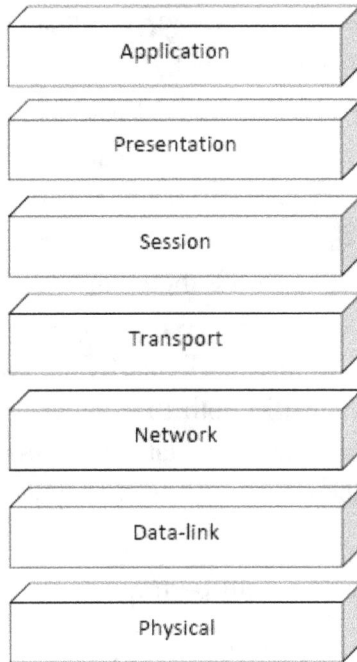

(Physical – Layer 1 up to Application – Layer 7 – in the OSI Networking Model)

# Layer 1: The Physical Layer

The first layer of the OSI networking model is the physical layer. This layer essentially defines the characteristics of the physical parts used in a typical network connection. For instance, in a network connection, the physical layer specifies the network cable, the router, the DSI/CSU box, and the other physical mediums involved.

The network cable transmits the data packet stream (in bits) from one node to the other in the physical network. Let's discuss this physical connection in a little more detail. The network connection established through this cable can be in either of the two forms.

- " Point-to-Point", a network connection established between two points.

- "Multipoint", a network connection established between several points, for example, a single point connecting to multiple other points.

The direction of transmission is also an important point of discussion in networking. This direction dictates the order of transmission, i.e., a data packet can be transmitted from one side of the network in one direction at a time. The sender transmits data received by the target, and only then can the receiver transmit data packets back to the sender. Hence data transmission is happening in opposing directions in turns). Similarly, in another type of data transmission on the network, both the sender and receiver can send and receive data simultaneously (data transmission is happening in both directions simultaneously). These two types of data transmission are called:

1. **Half-Duplex:** data can be transmitted only in one direction at a time.

2. **Full-Duplex**; data can be sent and received in both directions simultaneously.

The physical layer also specifies the method of bits transmission in the specified network. Transmission of bits in a network connection can be done in either of the two ways, i.e., **Series** or **Parallel**. Generally, the majority of network connections transmit bits serially, but the OSI networking model also accounts for the parallel transmission of bits.

To further clarify the physical layer's specification, here's a small list of metrics that generally fall into the category of this layer.

- The network cable being used
- The voltage being carried by the cable
- The measure of the electrical signal timing

- The distance through which optimal data transmission is supported by the network cable

# Layer 2: Data-Link Layer

The second layer of the OSI networking model is the data link layer. This layer defines those standards which give a sense of comprehension and value to the data packets or bits being transmitted and received by the physical layer. The data link layer of the OSI model bridges the connection between the third layer (network layer) and the first layer (physical layer) by defining and implementing a reliable protocol through which the network layer transmits its data through the physical layer.

The main purpose of the data link layer in the OSI model (besides linking the first and third layers) is to perform a data proofreading function. This is an informal and easy to understand way of describing the data-link layer's secondary job. According to technical standards, the data link layer performs detection and correction of errors within the outgoing data streams. In this way, the network ensures a reliable and error-free stream of data. Also, the data link layer features a term known as 'frames' that refers to the data elements that are carried by this layer. There are multiple frames, and some of the most commonly used ones are:

- X.25
- 802.x (includes Ethernet and Token Ring networks)

In the OSI networking model, the data link layer is further divided into two sub-layers. These two sub-layers are:

1. **Logical Link Control** (LLC)
2. **Media Access Control** (MAC)

Now, these two sub-layers collectively perform the main function of the data-link layer. This means that each of these two sub-layers individually performs separate tasks associated with the functionality of the data-link layer itself.

The LLC sub-layer establishes a link and controls it, i.e., call setup and termination along with transferring data. Due to this, the OSI model is compatible with networks such as telecommunication and LAN.

The MAC or Media Access Control sub-layer handles the assembly and disassembly of frames in the network, with addressing as well as error detection and correction. Now you can see these functions as the distinguishing characteristics of the data link layer itself.

Here is a list of some of the most common MAC protocols in the second layer of the OSI networking model.

1. 802.3 Ethernet protocol
2. 802.5 Token Ring protocol
3. 802.12 100Base-VBG protocol
4. 802.11 Wireless protocol
5. 802.7 Broadband protocol

Out of all these MAC protocols, the Ethernet and Token Ring protocols are the most common in computer networking.

# Layer 3: Network Layer

The third layer of the OSI networking model is the Network Layer. This is the layer where most of the crucial networking functions are performed.

There are several functions involved in this layer, but we will only discuss the major aspects which have a significant impact on the working of a network. Generally, the Network Layer determines the path or the route by which the data packet will travel from one node (point) to the destination point (node) on another network. The main job of the network layer is to define the route through which the data packets will travel from network to network.

Regarding the protocols used in the network layer, there are several, but the most important of them are the

- Internet Protocol (IP)
- Internet Protocol Exchange (IPX)

These protocols contain information which specifies the source and destination routing for the data packets. Hence, each network packet using these protocols can tell the network its destination based on the routing information from the protocol. After the data packet reaches its destination, this protocol also helps the receiving computer identify the source from where the data packet came.

The Network Layer holds significant importance in the OSI model for defining the transmitting of data packets from a single or multi-router setup. Before we discuss more details about these layers, let's also clarify the job of the router devices. A router is simply a piece of hardware designed to

- Examine each data packet
- Transmit the data packets to their intended destination by analyzing the source and destination address information

The Internet is a complex network, and a data packet being transmitted over the Internet might need to pass through several routers before it can arrive at its destination. But on a comparatively simpler and smaller network, the data packet might need to go through only a handful of routers or none.

When analyzing the network layer in a little more depth, an interesting point becomes clear. If the Network Layer is separated from the first (Physical) and the second (Data Link) layers, we realize that the protocols of this layer can function independently of these two lower layers. To put it into simpler terms, we can use the protocols of this layer in any variation and effectively use it with the lower layers without having to establish a chain of independence. For example, if the computers share a commonality regarding the first two layers, then the IP protocol and the IPX protocols can establish a network between these two computers. If we take this concept and apply it to a real-world scenario, then it would mean that a data packet using the IP protocol can be transmitted over an Ethernet, Token Ring, or even a wired cable connecting the computers. The same holds true for data packets using the IPX protocol, with the pre-requisite because the computers both support the IPX protocol and share a commonality in terms of the lower-level layers. In such a scenario, a network connection can be established.

# Layer 4: Transport Layer

The major concern of the transport layer is mediating the movement of data between the different layers. For this purpose, the transport layer masks the characteristics of lower layers from the upper layers in the OSI model. Besides this, the major functions of the transport layer include:

- **Flow Control:** directing the transmission of data between the sending device and the receiving device mainly to manage the influx of data that the receiving device experiences. The transport layer ensures that the receiving device is not flooded with more data than it can process.

- **Multiplexing:** divides a physical channel into multiple logical channels, which makes it feasible for multiple devices or applications to transmit data over one physical channel (or link).

- **Virtual Circuit Management:** Managing virtual circuits in a network in the sense of establishing, maintaining, and terminating the said virtual circuits.

- **Error Checking and Recovery:** incorporating the applications of multiple mechanisms to achieve the function of identifying data transmission errors and trying to rectify this error, for instance, issuing a request to the transmitting device to re-send or retransmit the data.

If we talk about the core purpose and functionality of the transport layer, then it would be essentially to handle the information flow that streams from one node to another node in a network.

Like the rest of the layers we have discussed up till now, the transport layer differs from them in the sense that for each operating system, implementing the transport layer is done differently.

The Transport Layer features a bunch of important protocols. Out of these protocols, the following two are used in connection with either IP or IPX data packets, respectively.

1. Transmission Control Protocol (TCP); used with the Internet Protocol (IP)

2. Sequenced Package Exchange (SPX); used with the Internet Protocol Exchange (IPX)

# Layer 5: Session Layer

The fifth layer of the OSI networking model is the Session Layer. By this layer, the model can define the connection established between two computers, either in a client-server connection or a peer-t0-peer connection relationship. The term 'session' is used to describe this virtual network connection between computers. Since the primary focus of the OSI model's fifth layer is upon these connections, hence it is named as the 'Session Layer.' the reason the establishment of a network connection between two computers is known as a 'session' is that once the connection is established, it persists for a certain period.

A session basically involves negotiations that take place between the connected client and the host. The points of focus in the negotiation are listed below.

- Flow control
- Transaction processing
- User information transfer
- Network authentication

# Layer 6: Presentation Layer

One of the higher tier layers, the presentation layer, is mainly concerned with presenting data in a form that can be comprehended by the system. The presentation layer of the OSI networking model collects all the data being supplied by the lower-tier layers. It then converts into a format that can be used by the system. Even though the name 'Presentation' may be misleading, the deliverance of data to be easily understood by the system is as important as the system presenting the data to be easily understood by the user.

The presentation layer performs these functions:

1. Data compression
2. Data decompression
3. Data encryption
4. Data decryption

From this, we can conclude that the main concern of the presentation layer is *data*.

# Layer 7: Application Layer

The last and highest tier layer in the OSI networking model is the Application Layer. If we analyze the nature of the interaction of each layer with their respective elements in a network, we can see a steady pattern. The layers in the OSI networking model begin their interaction with the physical elements within a network, i.e., the routers, network cables, etc. From here, the layers move toward interacting with virtual features and elements, i.e., moving toward intelligent aspects of the network. After this, the OSI model's focus on the virtual aspects of the network shift towards the involvement of the computer machine itself within the network, which is evident from the last two layers (Presentation and Application layers).

Continuing this train of thought, we can come to understand the purpose of the application layer in the OSI networking model and the overall working of a network involving computers. By doing this, we can analyze networks in a more detailed and comprehensive manner.

Now let's get to what the application layer is all about. The main concern of the application layer is to control and mediate the interaction of the network with the Operating System and the applications installed on this OS. It defines how the applications handle the communication that the system becomes involved in when connected to a network.

Examples of the software that fall under the definition of the application layer include:

- Windows Client for Microsoft Networks
- Windows Client for Novell Networks

Such software is typically used as a network client application in computer networks.

However, the data does not go through the OSI networking model in only one direction. It can go up the OSI model when the computer is at the receiving end of the network, and the data can go down the OSI model when the computer is transmitting the data through the network.

# Chapter 7: Network Security, Cybersecurity, and Hacking Methods

This chapter focuses on the basics of network security and recovery.

### Does network security play a vital role?

Internal security makes it possible for a person to protect their network from internal threats, which are more common than external threats.

A network's security is threatened by internal users in these ways:

- By accessing records of payroll and accounting, business development data, and other such information in illegal or inappropriate ways.

- Gaining access to another user's file which should have been inaccessible to others.

- Impersonating another user by sending e-mails under their name to cause mischief.

- Gaining entry into the systems and performing criminal activities that include embezzling funds.

• Letting viruses into the system, by accident or deliberately.

• Discovering user accounts and their passwords helped by sniffing packets.

Such internal threats must be eliminated by diligent management of the network's security. Among the many internal users in the network, at least some have the ability to exploit security holes in the network, and a few of these users might even try to do so.

# Account Security

In Account security, various tasks are carried out to manage the user accounts enabled on the network. To make sure that no security holes exist, a person besides the one managing the accounts should audit them often.

Management of the general account security requires these steps:

• The startup user account termed as 'Guest' in most network operating systems should be removed from the network immediately. Accounts used for testing, such as 'Test', 'Generic', etc., should not be created because these accounts are easy and frequent targets of crackers.

• The network operating system assigns a default name to the administrative account. It may be named as Administrator in Windows systems and Supervisor/Admin in NetWare. Change this name soon so attacks directed against the account can be avoided.

• Knowing how to remove access to network resources with quick precision from any user account and verify the network resources that contain their security systems. For instance, network operating systems and specific applications like the database servers or accounting systems handle the management of user accounts. Some systems don't deny access to deactivated or removed accounts unless they log out from the system, which can threaten security. It is necessary to discover how the system manages removed accounts.

• Establishing a relationship of mutual trust and working closely with the appropriate people in the Human Resources (HR) department is essential in maintaining proper security. By co-operating with the HR staff, you could work on the security issues related to the departure of employees and make a checklist for standard employment changes affecting IT. The HR department may not provide you with advance notices, but you must know about the terminations immediately for taking proper steps in time.

• Try to provide the new users with a program where they can submit their assigned permissions and have them reviewed and signed off by their supervisor. This step eliminates any possibility of these users gaining access to sensitive information.

# Password Security

Password security is an important aspect of account security, which enables you to set policies that control the time period within which the system forces the user to change their passwords, the complexity and length of these passwords, and whether old passwords can be reused. Password security policies should at least include these suggestions:

• Make sure that the users change their main network passwords every ninety to one hundred and eighty days through the network password policy settings. Even though thirty days is recommended, it can be considered too frequent for some environments.

• 'Reuse policy' should prevent users from reusing an old password for at least a year.

• Make a requirement that the passwords should be at least eight characters long. If the password being set is case-insensitive and does not allow special characters to be used, the possible variations of such a password are almost $36^8$ (three trillion). For case-sensitive passwords, the possibilities increase up to $62^8$ (218 trillion). If special characters such as space, comma, asterisk, period, etc. may be used in passwords, the possible variations increase even further.

• The users should be encouraged to use passwords that do not make up a word in any language or insert numbers and other nonalphanumeric characters between the letters of the word. In this way, a dictionary attack initiated by password-cracking programs will fail. Mixed-case characters should be used wherever the network supports mixed-case passwords.

• Policies that observe and detect numerous incorrect password attempts should be turned on. This policy is often termed *Intruder detection.* It monitors whether too many incorrect attempts at entering the password have occurred in a set amount of time and prevents further attempts by locking out the account. The locked account can only be reopened by talking to the administrator with the authority to reset the account. This case usually occurs when people forget their passwords, but this policy keeps in check any malicious intent to guess the password and gain access to the account.

• Novell NetWare and Windows servers can set limits on the amount of time a user can be logged in to the network, and restrict certain users to particular network computers. To impose these limits on every user would be too excessive; nonetheless, it is essential to restrict the administrative account to the fewest possible number of different workstations so a person operating at a different workstation cannot access the account even if they know the password.

According to the Catch-22 of network security policies, making the policies too strict can actually reduce network security. For instance, if the password security policies require the user to use a 12-character password, change it once a week, and prohibit the reuse of passwords, most users cannot remember the changing passwords. They will write it down somewhere in the office, with the risk of it being discovered.

To strengthen the security of the network, a balance must be maintained between security and usability.

# File and Directory Permissions

Internal security also involves the maintenance and control of users' access to files and directories. The settings related to this security are more difficult than managing the user accounts because every network user has at minimum 20 directories and hundreds of files, and managing this amount is a tough job. To make this task easier, the key is to follow regular procedures and periodically spot-audit particular parts of the directory tree that contain sensitive information. By effectively structuring the overall network directories, the top levels can simply be assigned permissions, which will "flow down" automatically to subdirectories and make identification of the users who have access to specific directories easier.

The settings related to assigning permissions on files and directories is considerably flexible in network operating systems. Various kinds of roles can be enabled for different users through built-in permissions. The roles mentioned below describe the authoritative ability of what the user can do in the directory:

- **Create Only:** This role gives the user the ability to create and add new files to the directory and prevents the user from accessing, altering, or deleting previously existing files, including those which they created. Helped by this role, the users gain permission to include new information in a directory to which they shouldn't have access otherwise. This role makes the directory function like a mailbox where one can only put new things in it, and only one other person will have full access to the content inside.

- **Read Only:** This feature allows users to see the files at a glance in the directory, and they can view these files on their computer. The read-only role only allows these users to view and read the information in the files, making no kind of changes. Such files can be copied via the read privilege by the users into another location or directory, which allows them to make desirable changes.

- **Change:** This feature gives the user a free hand with the files in the directory, which are inaccessible to other users.

- **Full control:** This role is limited to the owner of a directory who can make any alteration to the directory files and also can grant access to any other user as desired.

On different network operating systems, these features are designed in different ways.

Security for specific files can also be set in a way similar to setting permission for directories. The permissions assigned in both files and directories have similar workings. A user's ability to read, alter, or delete a file can be controlled for specific files, and Directory permissions are usually overridden by file permissions. This concept can be understood by considering a user has access to change the files in the directory. Still, once the permission is set to read-only for the files in that directory, the user can now only access the read-only feature.

## Practices and User Education

The people using the network are part of the reason for insecurity and internal threats. To make sure that the network remains secure and protected despite the threats, it is essential to develop effective security practices and habits.

Besides developing and implementing a good security practice or scheme, it is also imperative to manage it regularly by archiving the procedures related to security and establishing a process to ensure they are followed by the employees daily. A simple and comprehensible procedure easily followed is much better than the poorly followed complex yet excellent procedure. Therefore, the overall design of network security must be made simple while keeping it consistent with the company's needs.

Make it possible for all the users to follow prudent procedures. These procedures can be enforced by customizing the settings available on the network operating system, but formal education of the employees regarding the importance of internal security is also needed.

- Inform the users of the basic conditions they need to follow related to network security and provide them with a document containing the details of network security and the users' role in preserving it. The guidelines in the document for the user could be to choose a secure password and not disclose it, to take care not to leave their network-connected computers unattended for a long time, and to not install software from anywhere else other than the company.

- Discuss the network security issues with the newly appointed employees that will be using the network.

- Examine the company culture, and depending on that, consider making the users sign a form that acknowledges their comprehension of the security procedures they must follow.

- Auditing users' actions related to security should be done at certain intervals, and if some have full-control access to the directory, then keep a check on how they assign permissions to other users.

- Review the security logs on the network operating system occasionally, and if a problem occurs, investigate it properly.

Network security procedures are designed and implemented while keeping the worst-case scenario in view. Still, most of the time, security issues occur due to an innocent mistake or ignorance instead of malicious intent.

# Understanding External Threats

External security deals with protecting the network system from external threats. Before the Internet came into use, the procedures related to external security were easy to manage because the networks used only external modems to connect to the network. But Internet connectivity spread throughout the system increases the importance of external security and also the difficulty in managing it.

As long as the network is connected to the Internet, it can never be secure. Techniques that the crackers develop to overcome the security of a network are implemented via the Internet. The external threats faced by a network develop so rapidly that, if a book were written on all the current threats to a network, it would be out of date when it was printed.

The three basic external security threats are:

• **Front-door threats:** If an external person logs onto the network by guessing or cracking the password of one of the internal users, threats to system security arise termed as front-door threats. The intruder may have succeeded due to having a connection with the company or a personal relationship with someone using the network.

• **Back-door threats:** Back-door threats will arise if there are bugs in the software or hardware of the network operating system. The crackers take advantage of these bugs and breach the network security through them, then continue to find their way to the administrative account and finally taking control of the system. These threats can also be caused if the bugs are purposely programmed into the software of the system.

• **Denial of service (DDoS):** The DDoS attack can deny service to the entire network. A few examples include causing servers to crash by specific actions and increasing Internet traffic by useless data such as flood ping requests.

To counter the problem of crackers, several steps can be taken. These may not fend off the determined and highly skilled crackers completely, but they can make most of the crackers give up.

# Front-Door Threats

The most common threat is the front-door threats, where the external person gains access to a user account on the network. Some forms of front-door threats include a displeased ex-employee who had access to the network in time, or an outsider who guessed or cracked the password to a valid user account on the network or got it from the original user of that account.

The current or terminated internal users are more threatening to security because they have certain advantages of knowledge as compared to the regular crackers. They already know the crucial information required for cracking, such as the important usernames to target, other users' passwords during the time they were working together, the network structure, and server names.

Remembering this, internal and external security are interconnected, so if the policies and practices related to internal security are used, front-door threats are greatly reduced.

If the network resources that can be accessed from the LAN are kept separate from those that must never be accessed from outside the LAN, the risk of front-door threats greatly decreases. With providing the external user access to the accounting server, it is possible to manipulate the settings so the system cannot be accessed from outside the LAN.

Network resources can be separated and categorized based on the authorization to access these resources.

- Access to LAN from the outside should be controlled and given only to a specific type of people who need it among the traveling or home-based users. These users access the

LAN remotely through the Internet when you run the VPN software for them.

• If the users need to access the LAN remotely, consider creating remote access accounts for them besides their normal user accounts and set them to be more restrictive than the normal LAN accounts. This method is not generally practical, but the strategy used in it can prove helpful, especially for the users with broad LAN security clearances in normal times.

• The dial-back feature should be used for users that dial into the modems from a fixed location (such as their homes). In this feature, the phone number of the users' system from which they will dial in is securely documented. To connect to the modem, they will dial the system and request access. The remote access system ends the connection and dials the recorded phone number of that user. The user's computer picks up the call and establishes a real connection. In this way, the dial-back feature prevents access to the system if the dial-in phone number differs from the one recorded.

• Once the users with broad access to the system leave the company or are terminated, examine the user accounts to pinpoint the ones whose passwords are known by the ex-employee. After the employees leave, consider changing the passwords of such accounts immediately.

The people who had no kind of association with the company will often try an indirect method termed *social engineering*. According to this technique, they make use of a nontechnological method to gather information inside the company, including user accounts and passwords. Social engineering is most effective in large companies where the employees rarely know each other. One type of method is when a user receives a call from the outsider posing as the network administrator and is requested to give their password temporarily so a certain problem can be tracked down. Another method of the social engineering technique is by searching the trash documents and records for information that may help the culprit to crack a password. To avoid such threats, the employees should be specially instructed to deal with them and to be prudent about giving information over the phone as IT people usually never ask for anyone's password.

# Back-Door Threats

Problems and bugs existing in the network operating system or some other part of the network infrastructure (such as routers) are the main cause of back-door threats. Security holes are one problem that persists in all network operating systems and components. It may be effectively dealt with by staying updated with the software and security-related patches as they are released, and reviewing new information related to the security holes that may exist in the software.

Web servers should be made secure in these ways:

> • If you host the website associated with your company on an Internet Service Provider's (ISP's) system instead of your network, the server becomes more secure. The external server's good points include increased availability to the server (by providing services 24/7) and advanced security. Another point is that the concern related to allowing or disallowing LAN connections to the network from the outside is no longer relevant.

> • Ensure that a strong firewall router is configured and implemented for the system network. The firewall router you set up will be better off being tested by someone familiar with the workings of that firewall or who has helped with the configuration. Keep the software of the firewall updated.

> • Investigate the security settings related to the web server being used and confirm that they are properly implemented. By auditing these security settings periodically, the web server and the network remain secure.

- For the people accessing the web server from outside the company, create a web server that can be accessed from outside the firewall, or more precisely from between the firewall and the Internet router (demilitarized zone). This security method creates an obstacle for the crackers that invaded the webserver and will give them a hard time if they try to breach the network.

- E-mails are the most dangerous form of communication because they might be infected by viruses and Trojan horse programs. If the e-mail traffic is not monitored carefully, these might infiltrate the company network. This threat is prevented by using a virus-scanning software on the e-mail server and updating the virus signatures regularly.

# DDoS Threats

Another type of threat to the system network is the DDoS (Distributed Denial of Service) threat by which legitimate users of the network cannot obtain the network resources because they are denied access. It works in two ways, one of which is by flooding the network with useless traffic so the server (such as an e-mail server) denies services to the legitimate users or simply crashes under the heavy traffic load. The other way requires taking advantage of the existing bugs in the software of the network to crash the server.

Prevention of DDoS threats include:

- Checking and confirming if the network's software is updated and current.

- Firewall settings that allow the user to disable the Internet Control Message Protocol (ICMP) traffic service so traffic such as ping requests will not be allowed into the network.

- Not letting the people outside the LAN access those network resources and servers which they should not access.

For example, the accounting system of a company is made inaccessible to those outside the LAN because they do not need it. So, the firewall or packet-filtering router is configured so the traffic coming from and going outside the server's IP address is denied.

# Potential Attacks and Threats

A wide variety of malicious software exists in the computer world, and the list continues to grow. Some are listed below.

- **Viruses:** A computer virus is a code or program capable of copying itself and spreading by infecting numerous files such as COM, EXE, AND DLL program and application files. The document files for applications like Microsoft Word and Excel prone to virus attacks support macro languages, which are sophisticated enough to allow it. The data files, such as JPEG image files, are also at risk of being attacked by these viruses.

- **Worms:** The worm program functions by sending a copy of itself to other computers, which spread it to different computers after running it. The e-mail systems have lately been a victim of worms attached to e-mails in an enticing message. If the e-mail user opens the attachment, copies of the worm are spread to other people present in the user's e-mail address book. This action is carried out without the knowledge of the user, and the receivers of the worm face the same situation. In this way, worms spread like wildfire across the Internet through the e-mail server in just a few hours.

- **Trojan horses:** Trojan horse is a deceptive program that pretends to do something meaningful or of interest to the user but carries out malicious activities in the background during the period the user is busy interacting with the main program.

- **Logic bombs:** Logic bombs are malicious programming code pieces added into the normal program by the original author or by a person involved in developing the source code. They are set to become active after a certain amount of time, after which they delete key files and perform other malicious actions.

With each passing day, the already enormous number of viruses increases even more as new viruses are written and discovered. An important requirement of network administration is to establish practices to deal with these viruses.

Antivirus software runs on a network computer and monitors the software activities to search for potential virus threats. If a virus entity is discovered by the antivirus software, it protects the network by removing the virus from the original file while keeping it intact, and quarantines or locks it until an administrator checks it.

Antivirus is developed so it can run on most network computers, including desktop computers, file servers, e-mail servers, print servers, and computerized firewalls. Three most notable vendors among many that provide the services of antivirus are Symantec (Norton Antivirus), Trend Micro (PC-cillin), and Network Associates (McAfee VirusScan).

The most suitable option is to assure that the Antivirus is running on all the servers and customize the settings so its software is updated automatically.

As e-mail servers are more at risk of virus attacks, it is highly recommended to make sure that Antivirus software is running on them. The newly created viruses associated with e-mails can spread throughout the world in a matter of hours, so if you set the update of virus signatures to be on an hourly basis, you will likely get a necessary virus update before it attacks your network.

Running the Antivirus is also recommended on the workstations but depending only on this software to prevent virus attacks is not the right move. It should not be considered a primary way of dealing with viruses, but as a supplement to the server-based software.

# Basics to Hacking and Network Design

In this section, we will be discussing network designing and the basics of hacking. Network designing is a very important job best handled by network professionals. Designing a network from the ground up is time-consuming, stressful, and a very sensitive job. However, in return for carrying such a burden and responsibility, the resulting network built for the company is specifically tailored to their needs. This allows the company to work and function efficiently while using a network. Although network designing might seem intimidating at first, the process and philosophy behind it are actually simple and straight-forward once you get the hang of it.

Last but not least, we will lay the foundation for simple hacking by using the Linux operating system and briefly talk about the kill chain process of hacking that includes reconnaissance, exploitation, and such. However, clarify that covering even the basics of hacking is outside the scope of this book. Instead, we will focus on the major aspects.

# The Process of Designing a Network

Network design does not follow a scientific procedure, nor is it an exact science. That's why getting everything correct on the first attempt to design a network is virtually impossible, as every network has its own specific needs and demands that need to be met. Prominence and excellence in this task come from experience and practice. However, the trick to designing a good network is to estimate the needs of the network and then try to meet these needs to the best of your ability in the network design.

The network design process is not universal. It varies from person to person. Some processes are simple and easy, and some processes are horrendously complicated. In this chapter, we will learn about a network designing process moderately comprehensive yet very simple. There are only two steps to this process:

1. Assessing the network needs
2. Meeting the network needs

## Assessing Network Needs

Assessing the demands of the network is what will set up for good network design. Before we can even consider the specifics of the network design, such as the network cables, the topology, the operating system, etc., we must first understand the goal the network is supposed to accomplish. In the network design process, assessing the needs of the network should be given equal or more emphasis as the other steps.

Here are four questions that can give more than enough information needed in this step of the process:

- How much storage space do we need?
- How much bandwidth capacity do we need?
- What are the network services required in this setup?
- What's the maximum budget for the network installation?

After answering these questions, you will get the majority of the network demands. These sections provide a guideline on how to approach the network design process by assessing the network's needs.

## Applications

A productive approach towards assessing the network needs is to understand the applications supposed to be run on the network. The productivity of the network in helping its users defines a good network, and designing such a network is directly related to accurately estimating its usefulness. Most users on the network will be using software applications. Hence it is very important to make sure that the network supports these applications.

In networks, some applications are common among the different departments of a company, and some applications are specific to a certain department or a certain user. Here's a list of some applications commonly installed for all the users in a network.

- A Word processor
- A spreadsheet program
- End-user database
- A graphical presentation program
- E-mail application
- Anti-virus software

After listing the applications installed for every user, the person designing the network needs to determine how these applications will be used, and how often they will be accessed. For instance, a company of over 1,000 employees will likely have over 90% of its populace using a word processor. Now you just estimate the number of documents created by each user per month, the average size of the document, and the average storage time for each document (usually either dating to 2 years or indefinite). By making these educated guesses, we can estimate the demand of the users from the network based on the average size of the documents created by the users if they wish to transfer such documents over the network. You repeat this process of estimation for the other applications. By doing this, you will end up with a safe guess of what's the storage and bandwidth capacity required for the network.

Once we are done with the common applications, we move on to the department and user-specific applications. For new companies, this step is relatively hard. The person designing the network will be ambiguous about the applications used by the departments unless they are informed about it. Similarly, for companies around for a while, the network designer will already know these specific applications that the network must support. It is very important to know about the impact of each departmental application as it can have a considerable impact on the network. For instance, a department related to accounting will most likely revolve around shared database files. The network design for such a system must differ from the standard client-server design.

Here is a list of some of the most common categories of departmental applications.

- Accounting
- Distribution and Inventory control
- MRP or Material Requirement Planning
- IT
- Electronic commerce
- Human resources
- Payroll and stock administration
- Publishing
- Marketing
- Legal

Assessing these specific categories of applications is the same as the common applications.

# Users

Once we are done with estimating the application that the network must support, we can now work toward assessing the number of users that the network must also support along with the applications used by each user. Assessing the total is relatively easier. The company itself can provide this information, or you can infer it from their business plans and the long-range budget.

While designing a network, one should also factor in the growth capacity of the company, i.e., the network should be capable of supporting new users that join the company in the coming years. By studying the growth rate of the company, this demand can also be factored in while designing the network.

Besides estimating the number of users that will be on the network, we also need to factor in some important questions about the users, which have been listed below.

- **The Bandwidth Requirement:** Aside from the normal use of network services, does any user have significant bandwidth requirements?

- **Storage Requirement:** Are there any users with significant storage requirements besides the general requirement of the majority of the users? For example, if the electronic imaging department needs to catalog many documents into an image file format on the network's server, then how many users will need to access this cataloged data?

- **Service Requirement:** Are there any users in the company that need access to additional network services that most users normally do not? This question can be related to a group in a company that deals with sensitive data and needs to be partitioned from the rest of the groups on the local area network by using a network firewall.

# Network Services

While designing the network, consider the range of network services. For different companies, the requirement for network services is also different. For instance, if a company requires a simple network setup, then it might only need simple network services such as file and print services along with an Internet connectivity service. But a complex network setup will include many other network services. Here's a list of the network services that should be considered when designing a network for the company.

- File and print services
- Backup & restore services

- Internet connectivity
- FTP & telnet
- Web browsing and external e-mail services
- Internet security
- Remote access services
- DHCP services
- Centralized anti-virus services
- WAN services to other places
- Streaming services
- VoIP

There are three main aspects you must know for each of the network services.

1. The storage and bandwidth needed by each service.

2. Knowing the way these services will be provided to the users. Knowing the server that will host these services. Each server needs to be set up.

3. The network service requirement of the users or groups in the company. The company will not require every network service to be available for the users. Other times, there will be users or groups within the company that will need access to specific network services as opposed to the general populace of the company.

# Meeting the Network Needs

Once we are done with the assessment of the network requirements, the next thing to do is ensure these requirements are met. This step of the network designing process basically depends on the experience and resourcefulness of the person in charge of designing. There is no defined series of steps that, when followed, will give us a definite answer in what to do. Instead, you need to map the entire network to paint a portrait of what the network will be like. The foundation of this portrait will be the knowledge you have gained up to now in the assessment step of the network designing process. Another good practice is to seek feedback on your network design from networking professionals that have loads of experience in this field. Gathering advice from different critics and implementing it in your design may be the recipe for successful network design.

# The Basics of Hacking: The Kill Chain Process

The main focus of hacking is usually penetrating a network or a user account. The latter is simpler as several techniques can be used to approach hacking someone's account, such as using a brute force attack. In this book, we will discuss hacking regarding penetrating a network. However, we cannot cover every aspect related to hacking because an entire book can be written on this topic alone. Hence, we will only go through the main process of hacking, i.e., the Cybersecurity kill-chain process.

A Cybersecurity kill chain process has eight essential steps, and these are:

1. Reconnaissance
2. Intrusion
3. Exploitation
4. Privilege Escalation
5. Lateral Movement
6. Obfuscation
7. Denial of Service
8. Exfiltration

These eight steps are the very core and fundamental stages of a penetration attack by a hacker. No matter what type of attack you want to launch on a network, whether it be an internal attack or an external attack, you must follow through these eight phases to succeed in hacking.

# Phase 1: Reconnaissance

The first phase of the kill chain process is to gather information about the target. In this stage, the hacker's job is to simply observe the target and research information about the target through online resources. The attacker can look around the social media pages of the company it wants to target or go around gathering information about the company's employees from their social networking accounts. In modern days, researching a target is relatively easy, with so many resources at the hacker's disposal. An attacker determines the internal situation of the company itself by keenly observing it from an outsider's perspective. This reveals the potential weak links within the company's network that the attacker should target. During reconnaissance, hackers usually take either of two approaches:

- Passive Reconnaissance
- Active Reconnaissance

In passive reconnaissance, the attacker does not directly risk exposing his attempts to the target. Instead, he aims to gather as much information about the target as is available to the public and then to create links to other potential targets. For example, garnering an employee's name from the company's website, then looking up his social media accounts from his name, then figuring out his username, and the chain of investigation continues. The information gathered is publicly available, and this raises no alarms.

But in Active Reconnaissance, the attacker takes a more aggressive approach towards gathering information about the target. When following this approach, the attacker usually engages with the target system directly to figure out the potential vulnerabilities. However, doing so carries a certain amount of risk because the attacker's information-gathering attempts can be discovered by the target, and the attacker can then be exposed. Once the attacker has gathered information such as the names, titles, e-mail addresses of the target, the reconnaissance phase is complete, and he can now explore the different avenues through which he can proceed with the penetration attack.

## Phase 2: Intrusion

Once the attacker has gathered the information, he can devise a way that will give him access to the target's system. The focus of the attacker in this phase is to somehow get into the target's system by taking advantage of malware or security vulnerabilities. Once the hacker is inside the target's system, he can set up for the later stages of the kill chain process. After this, the information gathered from the reconnaissance phase will help the hacker to devise a believable and feasible attack, such as a spear-phishing attack. By sending a carefully constructed e-mail with a compelling context, an attacker can easily trick the target into clicking on a malicious link. This will give the attacker access into the target system and even more control of the system, i.e., by injecting spyware to gather passwords and other such information from the background without the target realizing. This phase of the kill-chain process is basically the entry-point of a penetration attack.

## Phase 3: Exploitation

In this phase of the penetration attack, the attacker infects the system with his own malicious code. This exploitation of the target system will essentially provide the hacker with better control over the target system. Exploitation needs to be done carefully. First, the target should not know the fact somebody has sneaked into his system. The exploitation phase mainly focuses on giving the attacker more resources to work with on the target system by exploiting the vulnerabilities discovered in the reconnaissance phase. An attacker can also install tools, create scripts, or even perform modifications to the security certificates of the target's system.

## Phase 4: Privilege Escalation

Sometimes, the target the attacker exploits has lower user privileges by default, or the attacker is only given lower privileges by the operating system after penetration. In such cases, it is of paramount importance for the attacker to elevate his access privileges in the target system. Otherwise, he will be locked out of most of the system's resources even after successfully penetrating it. In an analogy, privilege can be described in the following way. The attacker has successfully penetrated a building undetected and is now in the lobby; however, unless he escalates his privileges, he will stay stuck in the lobby, and that's practically useless for his objectives. Some of the most common approaches for escalating privileges are:

- **Brute force attacks** - this approach targets the password vulnerabilities to give the user administrator credentials, which can then access the system as an administrator rather than a standard user.

- **Exploiting zero-day vulnerabilities** - zero-day vulnerabilities are those weaknesses in the security of a system or framework present from day one of its development. The special thing about such a vulnerability is that neither the user nor the developer knows this potential flaw making the exploit attack virtually unstoppable.

## Phase 5: Lateral Movement

Now that the attacker has complete control of the system's resources, time to find the jackpot he came looking for. In this phase, the attacker will move from one system to the next in search of more data and assets. This phase is a sort of data discovery mission for the attacker. The goal is to find sensitive and critical data.

## Phase 6: Obfuscation

In this phase of the process, the attackers conceal their presence and cover their tracks. This will prevent immediate discovery of the attack and also make the future investigation of this attack more difficult. In this phase, the hackers usually delete metadata files, overwrite the timestamps, and make other such modifications.

## Phase 7: Denial of Service

In this phase, the hackers target the network and its corresponding infrastructure by temporarily dismantling it. In this way, normal users won't be able to access the network and won't know what's going in their systems and network. This is also commonly known as a DDoS attack.

## Phase 8: Exfiltration

This phase of the kill-chain process is the escape route of the hacker after he has gathered the data and information he came for. The main focus here is to somehow move the data from the target system to a system specified by the hacker, either by copying, moving, or transferring the data over the network. This process can take time, but once the data is out, the hacker can do anything he wants with it.

# Chapter 8: Useful Cybersecurity Tips for 2020

## Vital Function of a Disaster Recovery Plan

A disaster recovery plan is a document containing the step-by-step procedure of recovering a network after a disaster endangers the network data or hinders its functioning. The external financial auditors of a company need the annual disaster recovery plan to get the information listing the network data and its significance to the company, and repair the detrimental effects a network failure can have on the company network. While preparing a disaster recovery plan, the manager must carefully consider all the possible disaster scenarios and develop effective protection plans to prevent data loss and restore business operations quickly. Thus, the network Managers' two most crucial jobs include developing an effective disaster recovery plan and managing the backup systems of the company.

Most often, the disaster recovery plans are not long, although the length also depends on the complexity of the network's operations. Consider a single network with several hundred nodes and perhaps fifteen servers; the disaster recovery plan prepared for this network will only be around ten to twenty pages long. If a network is a complex like the Fortune 500 companies, the plan for disaster recovery of all the sites considered in aggregate may be several hundred pages long.

The usefulness of the disaster recovery plan can be maximized by making it concise and relevant while keeping some focus on even the remote problems that have at least a small chance of occurring. Pay attention to the results of the disaster, such as loss of a single server or an entire server room, or loss of all the customer service workstations, etc., instead of worrying about the causes that lead to this disaster.

The minimum issues that should be focused on in a disaster recovery plan are elaborated in the following section. Depending on the company and the network being used, other related issues might also need to be addressed.

## Assessing Disaster Recovery Needs

The disaster recovery plan should be drafted according to the needs of the company, i.e., the issues the plan should focus on and the person that requires the input into the process of recovery planning. Some other needs to be considered are:

- Considering various contingencies and formally planning for all kinds of possible disasters by designing countermeasures for them.

- Convincing the external accounting auditors of the company that a plan has been developed to counter the possible disasters.

- Making sure that the company's top management is notified about the risks and potential disasters, and the time it would take to deal with any problem that occurs.

- Developing a plan by starting from the key areas of the company's business considerations, including the different disasters related to the computer network.

• Persuading, the firm's customers that the data and operations of the firm are secure and safe from disasters.

Keeping these needs in view while planning will clearly show you what the plan should entail and which people from the different parts of the company should be involved in the planning process.

## Considering Disaster Scenarios

To effectively prepare for disaster scenarios, and develop a plan, consider many probable disaster scenarios such as:

• A fire breaks out in a room, such as the server room, and destroys some computers and tapes.

• The computer and backup batteries close to the floor of the server room are damaged by flooding. It can occur by an incident within the building such as fire sprinklers activating due to a fire, or a serious case of water leaking into a room near the server room.

• A problem in the electrical circuits occurs, causing the power to fail.

• Connection to the outside world is lost due to some problem like the critical Wide Area Network (WAN) or the Internet connection going down.

• The network or servers of the company face problems due to bad building structure.

• The computers in another part of the building, essential for running the company's operation, get affected by the preceding events. It could be one of the manufacturing areas, the customer service center, or the telephone system room.

The events mentioned above do not have a high chance of occurring. However, it is still imperative to consider them all because a disaster recovery plan is made to deal with serious problems. If the planning is focused only on the problems most likely to occur, it will be much less useful.

Some failures which could endanger the system should also be considered after planning for disasters:

> • The server's motherboard fails and a new one cannot be obtained from the vendor in less three days.

> • The failure of a disk causes the loss of data. If using the scheme of Redundant Array of Independent Disks (RAID), make a plan that accounts for failures worse than the RAID system can protect. Such as, if RAID 1 mirrored drives are used, create a plan that considers the failure of both sides of the mirror simultaneously. For RAID 5, consider planning countermeasures for when two drives fail simultaneously.

> • Consider a case where the tape backup drive fails, and repairs cannot be done within one or two weeks. This failure does not cause the loss of data, but it does increase the chances of such an event.

Planning for these failures requires ways of responding quickly and effectively. For example, if the server's motherboard fails, relocate the drives of that server to another one temporarily, until the motherboard gets fixed or replaced. If a disk fails, design a plan which contains a method to rebuild the disk array and quickly restore the data from a backup. If the tape backup drive fails, plan on how to obtain an equivalent drive soon, or if the tape-drive developer can make an exchange of the failed drive for a reconditioned replacement drive.

Consider keeping spare parts and backup servers so that in case of any failure, system operation can be resumed quickly. Examine what these responses entail:

> • Should a maintenance contract be kept close? If so, ensure that the guarantees and procedures are understood.

- Should spare parts be stocked and ready to use if a failure occurs?

- Is another computer available that can act as a temporary replacement for a key server if it fails? Can the same be asked for routers, hubs, switches, and other important components?

- Are the employees trained and ready to work with the replacements, or with no system if temporary measures have to be taken? For example, can a restaurant and its staff keep operating if the electronic system goes down?

- Is it necessary to maintain a hot or cold recovery site? A "cold" recovery site is a facility kept close to the protected data center and managed by the company. If the data center faces some disaster, the site can be hosted in this facility where all the power, air conditioning, and facility features are available. But the "hot" site has the same features as the "cold" site with the additional advantage of having computer equipment and software to perform the same processing as done in the data center. The data of the hot site is synchronized with that of the data center on a real-time basis, due to which it can take over the work of the main site in a short amount of time. Hot or cold sites are often used by those companies which need to carry out sensitive and mission-critical data operations.

The core of disaster recovery planning is based on two points; first, analyzing problems or potential risks, e.g., malfunctioning or failure of essential equipment, and second, after analyzing the risk managing it and overcoming the risk.

## 1. Handling Communications

The disaster recovery plan should cover the aspect of handling communication. If during a disaster, communication is not effectively planned, the people might not perform well at their jobs, and solving the crisis will be hampered.

Communication planning can be started by writing down the list of people that should be informed about a problem, how to track the progress made toward resolving it, and the result. An example list is given here:

- Board of directors
- President or chief executive officer
- Vice presidents of respective areas
- Supervisors
- Employees dealing with the problem

The next step includes deciding the notification that should be given to each person regarding the disaster recovery process. For instance, the board of directors may only need to be informed when the disaster progresses so much that it has a material effect on the performance of the company. But the supervisor and the employees directly affected by the problem need to be constantly notified about every development.

After considering the list of people and what they need to be notified about, decide the way they will be notified. If you are the one directly involved in solving the problem, consider passing on the responsibility of notifying the required people to another person not too directly involved so you can finish the process of resolution soon. This task should be delegated to your department's supervisor or an employee clear on the procedures required in communication. They should also have contact information such as home numbers, pager numbers, etc. if they must inform the person after working hours. Setting up a telephone tree will help to communicate with others quickly. The last task is to outline the order in which people are given the notification. This list depends on the company environment and the disaster, disregarding the organization chart of the company.

## 2. Planning Off-Site Storage

Off-site storage is a method of protecting data by keeping it in back-up tapes in an off-site place if a physical disaster like a fire destroys the copies of data present on-site.

Along with off-site storage of files, companies also provide standardized tape-storage practices that work on a rotation basis (most often weekly). The employee of the storage company visits the office and exchanges boxes by dropping one box of tapes and picking up the next set of tapes. The backup tapes are commonly contained in stainless steel boxes, and the duty of keeping these boxes locked and guarded is given to the network administrator. The decision as to which tapes to keep on-site and which to send off-site should be made carefully, like keeping the most recent backup tapes on-site and sending the older ones off-site. This is helpful, as you can keep the tapes you need daily close to you while reducing the exposure to disaster. Even if a disaster damages the server room and backup tapes, only the recent data will be destroyed, which does not amount to much loss.

## 3. Describing Critical Components

The plan developed for disaster recovery should also include all the computer equipment and software needed to keep the operations running should the entire building be lost. The roughly estimated cost of this equipment and the method of obtaining it quickly must all be a part of this plan. Such a list will help reduce the time lost in resuming the business operations in a temporary facility. The insurance purchases made against business operations will also be estimated in the total end cost.

## 4. The Backup and Restore Features of Networks

An inclusion that the disaster recovery plan for a network must have is the method of recovering the stored server data if it gets destroyed. One such method is establishing network backup and restore procedures. A network administrator should know the importance of keeping reliable backups of important data and the system itself.

When a person works with computers, it doesn't take long for them to notice the importance of keeping good backups, because computers can fail unexpectedly, making recovery of the data inside them impossible. Some files on the computer may also get deleted or corrupted due to an incident. If such cases occur, the company employees' jobs depend on the quality of backups for the destroyed data and the restoration of that important data.

## Assessing Backup Needs

Assessing the needs of a company's backup and restoration process comes before making the backup procedures for a network. To complete the assessment of backup needs, consider these questions:

- How dynamic is the server data, and with what frequency and in what ways does this change?

- What is data that needs to be backed up, and what is the growth rate?

- How much time does it take to make the backup of the data? Avoid a situation where you back up terabytes of data on a system that can only handle megabytes per hour.

- How quickly can a partial or complete restoration of data be done? Most often, the restoration of data takes twice if backing up the same data, though there are cases where the backup and restoration time is equal. For example, if the entire server took ten hours for backup, then the restoration data would be somewhere between ten to twenty hours, excluding the time needed to deal with the problem that led to having to restore the data.

- How much consistency in the backup data is required? Are the data files required to be managed as one unit? For example, the restoration of word processing files need not be coherent and will not impact other files in the system. However, a collection of database files from a high-end database is useful only if the files can be restored from the set from the same point.

- What compromise can be made between cost and recoverability? A backup system designed to backup files every minute can create high confidence in the fact there is no loss of data even if some issue arises. Such high-end backup systems are required in banks. But the cost and administration of such backup systems are high, and most companies might turn to some cheap alternative with a low degree of recoverability such as backup at off-hours (usually at night). A company can assess what it needs and how much it will spend.

- How many extra levels of backup are required by the company? The backups are mostly in tapes that support servers that use RAID arrays. In this way, the second level of protection is the tapes. Sometimes, multiple copies of the tapes are required, and each copy of the tape has a backup. Maximum redundancy can proceed by copying backups and keeping them at an off-site via some network connection.

When the assessment is to be made, the company's senior management must be involved. On a minimum level, the findings can be presented for seeking the agreement or input of the management.

# Acquiring Backup Media and Technologies

These factors should be considered when a backup system (hardware and media) is being chosen.

- Reliability
- Cost
- Capacity of storage

- Probable restoration frequency

- Fitting an entire backup into a single media

The following information relates to various backup technologies, their costs, and the pros and cons of each one. All the values such as prices of drives, media, and costs per megabytes, are based on approximations.

Digital Linear Tape (DLT) or Linear Tape-Open (LTO) are sturdy backup systems that should be considered if your company has adequate resources and ways of using their capacities. These systems are rated for re-use a million times, with a shelf life of 30 years. and have fast drives for backup and restoration. DLT and LTO can also have robotic autochangers, which make a lot of headroom if the drives are being filled up. These robotic autochangers are comparatively cheap, and various types are available, ranging from small systems with a capacity of five tapes to large systems holding tens to hundreds of tapes.

Super DLT S4 with 600GB per tape and LTO-4 with 800GB per tape are new backup technologies more advanced than DLT and are suitable for larger networks. A lot of computer equipment vendors support the tape formats of DLT and LTO and consider them to be reliable.

# Choosing Backup Strategies

The backup rotation strategy is planned after all the important information is collected, and this plan contains the details of how the backup media is rotated. Thoughtful designing of these backup rotations has these advantages:

- If a disastrous failure occurs, the system can be rebuilt based on the most recent data possible.

- If old tapes have been accidentally erased or damaged without being noticed they can have their files restored immediately before the data is lost.

- Provide protection if the backup media fails.

- Protect the data against cases of environmental disasters like a fire.

The files on most network operating systems have special bits assigned to them, one of which is called the archive bit, and it specifies the backup status of the file. The archive bit is set to 'on' whenever a file is edited, indicating the need for a backup of this file. Once the backup is done, the archive bit clears. With archive bit and backup software, the backups that can be created are:

- A **full backup** in which all the files and directories are backed up with no regard to the statuses of the archive bits. This method clears up all the archive bit on every file in the backup.

- An **incremental backup** selects those files modified and had their archive bit on, and then creates backups for these files. The only files backed up are those that have been edited since the last incremental or full backup, and their archive bit is reset; those who have not been modified will not be included. Though the time consumed in incremental backups is minimized in each daily backup, the restoration time is increased, and the possibility of media failure becomes high.

- A **differential backup** works by backing up those files which have their archive bits set to on. The change in this backup is that the archive bits of the files are left on even after a backup so that in subsequent backups, they will be backed up repeatedly along with other new modified files. The time taken in performing backups is increased, but the restoration time, and the possibility of media failure, is reduced.

Ideally, performing full backups is advantageous as you have to access only the most recent backup tapes to restore the system if a failure occurs. Looking at it realistically, such a thing is not feasible due to several reasons. First, to perform a full backup is time-consuming, and there may not be enough time to do a full back up daily. Second, the less work is done by the tapes and media, the more shelf life they will have. Besides these concerns, consider much restoration time the combination of a full and incremental or differential backup will take along with the risk of being unable to restore the data due to using a combination approach. Also, consider the scenario where you need a full restoration, and you have to use one full backup tape and four incremental backups used since then. All the five tapes need to be in good condition, which is less likely than encountering a bad tape.

It is common to mix the backup types by performing one full back up in a week and using the incremental or differential backups for the rest of the week. Some examples are:

- **Full back up Friday nights and incremental backups from Monday to Thursday:** Due to system failure on a Monday morning before any data entry, only the Friday's full backup needs to be restored. But if the failure happens on Thursday, four tapes need to be restored in sequence for a complete backup, starting from Friday's full backup and continuing from Monday's incremental backups till Wednesday. In the second case, all the data in those tapes must be restored successfully and sequentially to ensure data integrity. If it is not done, the files might become mismatched and hard to use. Hence four points of media failure in the form of tapes increase the risks more than you can handle.

- **Full back up Friday night and differential backups from Monday to Thursday:** if system failure on Monday morning occurs, only previous Friday night's full backup restoration is needed. But if it fails on a Thursday Morning, complete restoration of data required only two tapes: the previous Friday's full back up with the differential backup done on Wednesday. This is because, in the differential backup, all the modified files since the last backup have been backed up, and so, the number of possible media failure points decreases due to only two tapes needing to be restored.

A good backup scheme needs a balance between the data's nature and the risks with each backup, the tapes' capacity, and the time consumed in each backup.

The 'Grandfather-father-son' (GFS) scheme is the most common backup rotation scheme. Eight tapes are used in implementing this scheme. Four of these tapes are named from "Monday" to "Thursday," while the other four are "Friday 1", "Friday 2", "Friday 3," and "Friday 4". The first four are used from Monday to Thursday to replace the data from the previous week, while the next four tapes are designated for each Friday in the month. For the first Friday in the month, use the "Friday 1" tape and so on. Prepare a month-end tape on the last day of each month, not for being re-used but for keeping it off-site so it can be used where a crisis like an environmental failure destroys the system and all the on-site tapes.

GFS has three main variations:

1. Perform a full back up each time, which increases media redundancy but reduces restoration time.

2. Perform full backups only on Fridays and the end of the month, and during the rest of the weeks use incremental backups.

3. Perform full backups on Fridays and month ends, and during the weeks perform differential backups.

Compared to GFS, rotation schemes are simpler; only two or three tapes can be used by rotating them in a sequence and overwriting the old data each time. In this way, the three previous days' data can easily be restored. But it is impossible to retrieve data from further back in time if it was erased or damaged with no one noticing immediately. A way of solving this shortcoming is by using several more tapes that can be rotated weekly or monthly.

# Conclusion

Until now, we have covered a variety of topics related to computers. We have comprehensively discussed computer networking because it is very relevant in our modern age ruled by the Internet. We have learned about the OSI networking model and how the different protocols and networking applications adhere to this model. After addressing computer networking, we shifted our focus toward network security, which is a very important topic to discuss as nobody wants their data to be compromised and misused. In the final portion of this book, we have given due importance to topics such as network designing and hacking, with the latter being more interesting and informative. Hacking is something anybody with the right tools and knowledge can do. This book has explained the general process of hacking, which is commonly called the 'kill chain process.' the book has given readers the best of each topic and hopes that the readers have developed a basic conceptual foundation of each topic discussed in this book. When studying any material that relates to the topics covered in this book, the reader will have enough background knowledge to readily digest information meant for an intermediate or advanced-level audience.

www.ingramcontent.com/pod-product-compliance
Lightning Source LLC
Chambersburg PA
CBHW050644190326
41458CB00008B/2414